Who Does What and Why
in Book Publishing

Who Does What and Why in Book Publishing

Clarkson N. Potter

A Birch Lane Press Book

Published by Carol Publishing Group

Copyright ©1990 by Clarkson N. Potter

A Birch Lane Press Book
Published by Carol Publishing Group

Editorial Offices
600 Madison Avenue
New York, NY 10022

Sales & Distribution Offices
120 Enterprise Avenue
Secaucus, NJ 07094

In Canada: Musson Book Company
A division of General Publishing Co. Limited
Don Mills, Ontario

Manufactured in the United States of America

Library of Congress Cataloging-in-Publication Data

Potter, Clarkson N.
  Who does what and why in book publishing / by Clarkson N.
Potter.
      p.   cm.
  "A Birch Lane Press book."
  Includes bibliographical references and index.
  ISBN 1-55972-056-5 (paper) :
  1. Book industries and trade—Vocational guidance.   2. Publishers
and publishing—Vocational guidance.   3. Book industries and
trade.   4. Publishers and publishing.   I. Title.
Z278.P63   1990
070.5'023—dc20   90-41899
                                                          CIP

This book is for Helga

Contents

7

Acknowledgments

A book such as this is the result of a long and, at least in my case, sometimes painful education. To try and thank the many people who contributed to the store of what I know would be to list dozens if not hundreds of names, and so I shall here limit myself to thanking explicitly those people who were especially helpful in the preparation of this manuscript. For that I am very grateful and thank Professor Barry Beckham, David Black, Walter Bradbury, Bud Cartter, Jeanne Chappel, Kate Condax, Ruth Anne Evans, Mike Gladstone, Professor Virginia Held, the staff of the Jamestown Philomenian Library, Alan Kellock, Diana Klemin, Judy Krantz, Jane Pasanen, Jean Peters, Miriam Phelps, Bill Ray, David and Ellen Seham, Tim Seldes, Peter Skolnik, Elizabeth Tilyou, and Dick Wincor. Kathleen Fogarty, Jennifer Hokanson, Denise Knight and Evangelos Pallis all read an early version of the manuscript and their suggestions were almost all acted upon. Erwin Gilkes carefully went over the entire manuscript twice and much improved it. Special thanks are due in addition to my editor at The Birch Lane Press, Sandy Richardson, and to all of his capable staff.

Preface

THE IDEA FOR THIS BOOK developed from the lessons I learned while teaching a course entitled An Introduction to Publishing before two quite different groups. The first was a large group of mostly seniors in the English Department together with a few graduate students in the Writing Program, who were both attending Brown University. The other group was a small number of adults who had enrolled in the Continuing Education program at The Rhode Island School of Design. They included among others a professional librarian, a poet, a newspaper reporter and a retired printer. In each case, however, they were interested in the same questions— what gets published and why, and how does the system actually work? At Brown, many were hoping to make careers in the business, while at RISD, most were interested in more abstract and theoretical questions.

For both these groups I searched for books that would help me in my teaching, and read everything that seemed relevant to the needs of the course. What I found was that there are good books in three areas of publishing, namely in its history, in its graphic design and artistic aspects, and

11

in its precise methods of production, including printing, papermaking, binding and all the rest.

The only books that were available that at least seemed to cover the subject in an overall way—and the ones that I assigned to my students—were all received with boredom and often with irritation, as the students felt that they did not address any of the central questions that they wanted to know about. My survey of these books is the basis for the bibliography that is included at the end of this book— an effort to fill a gap that existed then and now, and not intended to be a text, but to answer the questions that seem to be at the heart of what might be called the mystery of publishing.

This book concerns itself only with the points at which decisions are made in publishing, and deliberately leaves out all of the mechanical aspects of the business. It centers on the authors, the editors and the publishers themselves. Together, these three people make all the important decisions that bring a book before the public, and it is to their training, their aims and motives, and their daily interactions that we must look to begin to understand the answer to the question—what gets published and why, and how does the whole process actually work? By looking at what goes into each decision as it is made along the way, we shall, I hope, discover that what may seem irrational when viewed from the outside, is in fact nothing of the kind, but the result of much trained and careful thought.

Writers, editors and risk-takers have all been with us in the book publishing business for as long as there's been one. Many of these have been and remain quite intelligent people who have the same goal—to disseminate their ideas and their writings, and to make money while acquiring a public. The result of all those years of trial and error is now a very complex system that nonetheless manages to put before the American public in excess of forty-five thousand new book titles every year—or much more than any one person could possibly read. It is not a system governed by caprice—or at least it isn't most of the time.

This book, therefore, will examine the inner workings of decision makers in the book business, with two hopes in mind. The first is to make easier the jobs of the people who are now involved with the business by increasing the respect the major players in the game should have for each other. The second is to increase the understanding of the people who are now outside looking in by offering them some insight into the motives of the people who are in the game—motives that are seldom if ever explained but which actually constitute the unspoken but perfectly real rules of the game.

Who Does What and Why
in Book Publishing

I

Writers in the
Publishing Process

Introduction

IF YOU WERE TO ASK ANYONE in publishing whether
writers are born or made, most would answer that writers are born. To the people in publishing, writers are
presented as is. Editors are not in the teaching business,
but only in the selection of talent and the nurturing of it.
Who do they select and nurture?

To the people who want to be published but cannot find
a publisher, no matter how often they send off their cher-
ished work, the whole business seems like some mute
stone castle whose only purpose is to repel their feeble
attempts at rushing the gate. They have been told that
only published writers will be considered, that first novels
are never accepted, or they run up against any of dozens
of other dodges that make the task of finding a publisher
appear impossible. They always keep trying, signing up
for mail-order writing courses, enrolling in creative writing programs, laboriously turning out copy and sending it

forth, reading all the books published about how to write well—and only a few of them ever make it.

Whether or not writing can be taught is a question that keeps coming up in literary circles. To anyone in publishing, the most that can be expected is that someone with genuine native talent can be taught how to write *better*. There are so many publishers and so many people who want to be published that the truth is that too many people are published who never should be. When marginal writers are in fact published, it only encourages those who are submarginal, so publishers keep being sent incredible masses of unreadable stuff, and finding the actual talent is only that much harder. This book does not concern itself with the people who do not find a publisher, but with the ones who do.

As we shall see in this section, we will consider writers not as isolated creators whose tasks are over as soon as they type their last page, but as integral parts of the publishing process itself. From our point of view, their involvement with publishing doesn't end with a finished manuscript, but only then begins. Writers may be the originators of the book, but they are also the first essential player in the small drama that constitutes the making and the selling of each new book. It is thus as a pivotal actor in this drama that we consider the writer's role in the whole publishing process, and his or her integration into the complex chain of events that makes for complete and successful publication.

Most published writers had little or no trouble finding a publisher, and many if not most of them did so early on. Becoming a writer is a process that usually starts in the early teens with a preoccupation with books, stories and reading, and, as with most artistic preoccupations, it never lets up. Most writers know that they want to be writers by their middle or late teens. For some it comes very easily and naturally, while for others it requires much application and the conscious learning of a craft. In either case, the only way the writer progresses is by doing a lot of writing. If there is any real talent, it will be recognized by peers and teachers in high school and college, and practice and encouragement will come early. By the time the young person gets to a publisher, someone with some background and experience, most often a teacher, but sometimes another writer or merely a discriminating friend, will have noticed a spark. It is extremely rare for a writer to come out of nowhere.

The best writers write out of some inner compulsion that keeps them at it. Of course, there are those who want fame, or money, or influence over other people's ideas, and some achieve all these goals, but even they will at some point have turned from being young people with natural talent into professionals who think of themselves first and always as writers doing a job of work. As far as any outsider is concerned—including their editors—they are a self-selected group, and no two are alike, although they all do share the basics, a native talent coupled with a willingness to do hard and sustained work. For most the rewards are and must be psychic—even for the ones who profess to do it for nothing but money or the ones who will tell you that they hate writing. The most cynical or the most reluctant are kidding themselves, because if there was no inner reward at all either they wouldn't do it, or if they did, it wouldn't sound right. Once the words are on the page, they say what they say, and if the writer himself does not understand fully their import, others will. In short, whether or not they admit it, writing must give satisfaction to its creator. When it does, it may well give satisfaction to many others, and so a writer may find readers. To do that effectively, the words need to be published.

Writers

Book publishing is a complex, organized system taking a writer's words and getting them into the hands of as many readers as possible. It is of the essence that writing consists of an activity carried out by one person alone and that reading is also done by one person alone. Everything that happens between these two acts can either help or hamper the basic transfer, but book publishing is structured with the aim of having the writer's work become read by as many people as can be found. Here we will treat the writer as his publisher sees him, as the vital originator of what the two together do, and as the most important partner in the long process of finding and satisfying readers.

For a great many writers, everything starts with their being taken up by an editor and discussing their contracts. Since the contract itself is so central to everything that happens in publishing, we need to pause at this point and take a look at what it is and what it means.

The entire edifice of publishing is reared upon the law of copyright. After the invention of movable type made multiple images cheap and available, everyone concerned with printing had an interest in controlling what was printed and how it was disseminated, not to mention how the money from the sale of printing was to be allocated. Authors wished to control the accuracy of the reproduction of their words and to receive royalties from printers. Kings and bishops wished to control what people read so that heresy and sedition would not be presented to them freely. Printers and publishers sought freedom as well as monopoly rights in some works. The first formal copyright law was passed in England in 1710, and all laws since then have had the same basic effect, which is to give the author of a work control over who prints it for a specific number of years. Thus all publication of books may be viewed as taking place under a license granted to a publisher by an author and specifying exactly what is granted, on what terms, and for how long. This agreement between the originator of a work and a publisher is called the book publishing contract, and it is essential for authors as well as people everywhere in publishing to understand and be familiar with the fundamental provisions of any contract. We will, therefore, consider them in their basics.

Fundamentally, a book contract is a grant of the right to print and to sell copies of an author's work. The grant can be and is limited to a specific time and a specific territory—the time being usually the term of copyright and the territory the world or some part of it. Subsidiary grants may be made by the author directly, as in the case of foreign language editions, or by the publisher who acts as the author's agent in placing those subgrants and handles everything. It is of the essence that this grant is exclusive and that both the author and the publisher will defend this exclusivity in court if need be. It is thus the grant of a monopoly to print and sell, and in return the publisher grants the author a continuing interest in that monopoly in the form of the payment of royalties for the sale of copies of the work and the other rights that accrue to it. The details of those payments and their scales are the everyday concern of authors and their publishers, who negotiate them at the time of signing the original contract. They form the core of what is agreed to at the outset.

In order to make the contract workable, the publisher asks the author to warrant several things, that is, to assure the publisher of them on pain of abrogating the contract if those assurances are not true. These are that the author has in fact written the work, that he has not contracted for it elsewhere or caused its common-law protection to be breached so that he no longer owns the work, and that the work is completely and solely the author's and done by no other. This is central to the contract and to the power of the author to enter into it. In practice, of course, it means that the author promises that he has not plagiarized someone else's work to produce this one. No publisher's editor can possibly have read everything, and thus cannot be expected to spot lifted passages in some new book. Therefore, publishers naturally do not want to have the nasty surprise of someone turning up and claiming that he was in fact the writer who wrote something the publisher has now put out under another author's name. This leads to lawsuits, settlements for damages, and sometimes the withdrawal of an entire edition. It also happens occasionally that a writer, stuck for a passage he cannot produce easily for himself, lifts something out of another book, usually some rather obscure other book, and just slips it in as his own. The people who spot this are rarely the publisher's editors or lawyers, but invariably the damaged party—who sets up a loud howl as soon as he or she finds it out. The warranty is thus an elementary protection to which both sides easily agree for obvious reasons.

The author's assurances do not end there, for he usually insists that he has not defamed or libeled anyone else and that what he has produced is "lawful." This once meant that it wasn't pornographic during times when works that were deemed to be such brought charges against publishers, charges that could be not only expensive but often indefensible. Nowadays, book publishers are not much prosecuted for printing pornography, so there is little that can be unlawful, but there is still libel, and people still do bring libel suits. In the case of *Time* magazine and Ariel Sharon, the suit was tried and cost everyone concerned massive sums—so a libel suit is not trivial, no matter what the outcome. The warranties that the author gives the publisher on this score are therefore of some moment, and every contract should spell out in detail exactly what happens and who is responsible for what in the case of a suit brought against the book and its publisher. It happens quite commonly that a weak suit is brought against a book and the publisher wants to get rid of the suit cheaply by settling it, but the author, outraged that his reputation is impugned, wishes to pursue it and vindicate his name. At this point, what happens? If the eventuality has been spelled out in the contract, all goes as each party wishes, but if it has not, there can be a terrible mess, which can actually lead to a secondary suit between the publisher and the author. Well-drawn contracts anticipate this sort of thing and provide for various events before a crisis has arisen.

In exchange for the author's delivery of his work, his grant of rights and his warranties, the publisher agrees to publish the work at his own financial risk and expense. This then is the essence of his agreement with his author. The publisher assumes the commercial risk and has no recourse from the author if this risk should prove costly. The author gets his royalty on each copy sold whether or not this is a profitable sale for the publisher. We shall hear much more about royalties later on, but at this point it is only appropriate to observe that, in theory, the author's royalty account is always in his favor.

After these basic points have been agreed upon, the contract then goes on to spell out in detail all the other matters that have to be covered by the undertaking, the royalty rates on different kinds of sales, the disposition of subsidiary rights, what happens with respect to payments and accounting, the reversion of rights if the book is out of print, whose laws prevail, and any number of other relevant matters. Some of these things will come up again in later sections where they are of interest, but for now it is best to leave the details alone. It is the basic agreement that counts.

We will now go back to a consideration of what happens when a writer has been taken up by an editor, has signed a contract, and is ready to enter the publishing process itself.

Agents

Before we do this, however, it is necessary to pause and consider the matter of writer's agents, for many writers find that agents are useful if not absolutely necessary to get to the point of being offered a contract. At the outset, writers may have as much trouble finding an agent as they do finding a publisher, perhaps more, as agents usually handle only a small number of writers who get published regularly. Actually, an agent is a help in direct proportion to how lucrative a book can be to an author—that is, the more money it might make, the more it needs an agent. Thus a novel that stands a chance of getting a book-club sale, a paperback sale and even a movie sale certainly needs an agent. But a guide to antiques, say, is another matter. For that kind of book, there is not very much that an agent, however well meaning, can do to increase its income.

An agent's commission is generally 10 to 15 percent of everything that comes in from a given work. The author thus gives up that much in the expectation that, because of the agent's knowledge and effort, he will earn that much more than the commission costs, and will end up with far more than if an agent had not been involved. As a rule, one would have to say that if an author doesn't think his agent will get him at least 20 percent more than he could get by himself, then he doesn't need him. If, however, an agent can double an author's earnings on some book, then the author would be foolish to do without him. The agent himself, of course, must make the calculation as to whether it is worth his time to handle any given work. Say that a given deal takes him six phone calls to arrange. If he makes those calls and ends up with a thousand dollars that the author might not have otherwise, his cut hardly pays for his time. If the same six calls increased the value of a contract by ten thousand dollars, he has done a good day's work. For him as well as his author, he must think with the mind of a lawyer, as all that he has to offer is his special knowledge and his time.

If an author does have an agent, though, it is well for him to remember what the agent can and cannot do for him. Few agents are either literary critics or editors, and should never be asked to be. The agent is most useful in getting the best contract possible, and that includes a lot of things that are not strictly money matters. Can he, say, get an advertising guarantee from the publisher? Publishers don't like them and rarely offer them, but can be persuaded if they want a book enough. This doesn't increase the author's take directly, but it certainly is a great ego boost, and is the kind of clause that only an agent is likely to be able to get.

An agent can also protect an author from hidden contract pitfalls that the latter may know nothing about, such as there being no limit on the amount a publisher may hold back in royalties due "as a reserve for returns." Some authors think that the mere vetting of a proposed contract in a careful and knowledgeable way is worth paying the agent's percentage. I would question whether well-known publishers' contracts are so full of pitfalls for authors, but I have seen contracts that were offered by smaller and lesser known companies that were so bad that only a complete innocent would sign them.

All publishers' contracts are written initially as a document that is to their benefit. If the document should come back signed just as it was sent out, so much the better for them. The fact is that a large number of author's contracts do come back without any changes or questions. Not only are many authors glad to get a contract but also tend even to lack interest in reading and thinking about legal language in small type. Publishers thus get a lot of concessions as a matter of course from authors without agents while at the same time being perfectly amenable to the many changes that any agent might insist on. This does not mean that an author should always have an agent. It does mean that every author without one should do his own homework and find out what is customary and proper and what is not. It is not all that bad an idea to start with a contract written as being ideal from the author's standpoint—the Authors Guild contract, for example. It might be worth noting that the authors probably did themselves little good in drawing up and promulgating that document. It is so unremittingly and obviously hostile to publishers and so adversarial in its spirit that I know of some publishers who will at once withdraw an offer for a proposed contract if an author insists on starting with it. The problem arises from the Authors Guild lawyers making the assumption that every concession an author gives a publisher is of value to the publisher and that every concession a publisher receives results in profits. As we will see in detail later, since this is the case in far less than the majority of books, any contract based on those assumptions bears little relation to reality. Nonetheless, I suggest it as a means of finding out where the other extreme is from the publisher's printed contract. If what ends up being signed is about halfway between, then it is probably fair.

It should also be remembered that there are certain things about which publishers feel very strongly and some about which they do not, and only an agent or someone who is dealing regularly with them is likely to know what they are. One example is the jacket of the book. Inside every publishing house it is felt that a jacket is one of the major selling tools of the publisher's whole presentation— it is a poster for the book, and as such it is advertising. Since it is part of the publisher's selling effort, and part of his commercial competence to make it as effective as he can, the last thing he wants is some amateur poking his nose into how the jacket is designed. The writer may be a professional when it comes to writing, but is not necessarily so when it comes to advertising and promotion, so some houses never show authors a jacket sketch. Often, the first time the author sees it might be in the catalog listings, or in *Publishers Weekly*, or in some cases not until he finally sees a finished book. This is, of course, carrying things a little too far, and it has led to some very bad jackets. Just before sales conferences, every publisher will be knocking out a bunch of jackets and in the rush a few of them will be lousy. If the salesmen don't object, and they seldom do, a particular jacket may well be kept and then the poor author finds himself stuck with a book that has a jacket he hates.

One of my friends wrote a very good novel, went to the bookstores to see it when it came out, but couldn't find it. It turned out that the publishing house had been so occupied with other features that the title of the book was underplayed. Looking at the jacket from even a few feet away, one found it impossible to tell what the title of the book was. I tried finding it myself in a couple of stores, and discovered that even though there actually were copies in the stores, even I, who knew what to look for, could not find the book. The author was devastated. His book was a disappointment for the publisher. A clean, readable and simple jacket certainly would have made a big difference in the sale. But the author had no say in how it looked. A smarter publisher would have made certain that an author got a look at design proposals before proceeding. If the author had said, "But where is the title?" then some revisions could have been made in time. In any case, the publisher generally doesn't want to give the author contractual right of approval of the jacket—that is giving up too much to someone who is usually an amateur. If the author happens to be an advertising or promotion executive, then of course he will be shown the jacket, but even then the publisher will not want that right to be a formal part of the contract.

It cannot be expected that, even if he does do his homework, an author will know how strongly a publisher will feel about any given point, and that is why the first thing that must be established is a good working relationship between author and editor. The editor should explain how touchy the house is on author approval of jackets and why it should not be part of the contract, but will make certain the author sees the jacket sketch and will discuss it before anything is made final.

It should be remembered that for everything about which the publisher feels strongly there will be something else about which that he couldn't care less. For the author it is a matter of knowing what he cares about, working with his editor, and always being reasonable.

In sum, an agent is useful and necessary in direct proportion to how much a book can be promoted. Almost all novels benefit from promotion, whether they are from a new writer or a veteran, and a novelist definitely should, in my view, have an agent. Anyone who is publishing a textbook called *The Dynamics of Nutrition*, or is delivering a manuscript on *How to Collect Art Deco*, can safely manage without one. The writer must consider where he stands between these extremes, and make his choice accordingly.

Lawyers

Many writers who do not have agents decide that before they sign a contract they should show it to a lawyer. Unfortunately, they often show it to a lawyer who has no experience with book contracts, and the authors find they have paid a fee without getting the protection they want. All editors have had to waste time with lawyers who clearly know nothing about the literary business, and whose questions are almost never to the point. Their ignorance is often accompanied by an exalted sense of their importance and an assumption that they are involved in an adversarial proceeding. Thus, not a few authors find that the atmosphere has been given a bad odor before they even meet their editor. My own very strong advice to an author is that if you think you need a lawyer before you sign a contract—and I have never had a quarrel with that position—just be sure that you find a lawyer with some experience with book contracts or literary property in general. The book I published entitled *Literary Property* was written by Richard Wincor, a lawyer, and obviously I recommend it. Just remember that your mother's friend who does trusts and estates isn't going to be of much use in the publishing area.

29

In dealing with an agent, a writer should always remember a few simple rules. The first is that an agent is like a lawyer in being able to arrange a prospective deal and to recommend acceptance, but it is only the writer himself, like the lawyer's client, who can say yes or no. With an agent and/or a lawyer, the writer can never find himself stuck with a deal to which he didn't agree or turn down an offer without knowing it. All legitimate offers must be reported to the writer even if the agent thinks they should be turned down. The agent, then, can never act as a principal. This, oddly, is a point that many writers seem to forget and one hears of them being unhappy with deals that they say their agent made for them. The truth has to be that they accepted the deal themselves, only now they think they could get a better one, so they shift the blame to the agent.

As the agent can never make a deal without the agreement of his writer, so the writer should never try making deals without his agent. Never go behind your agent's back. If a writer meets someone from another publishing house at dinner, he must restrain himself from discussing the terms of the deal that his agent is just now trying to work out with his regular publisher. All outsiders, when asked, will be glad to offer advice, and may even be willing to offer a deal, but such things only make serious negotiation impossible for the agent. Any offer or deal that comes up outside the agent's purview should be reported to him at once. Only if the agent is fully informed can he be expected to make the best of any given negotiation. Many writers think they are better negotiators than their agents, and so try and do his work for him, but this invariably produces a mess.

It is also sad but true that many writers resent having that percentage come out of everything after a deal is made. In the view of many writers, an agent made a few phone calls and fixed up a deal that virtually any school-boy could, and now skims off the top forever. The writer feels that the agent really didn't do enough to justify his take, and so he often tries at that point to get rid of the agent. This is, of course, a betrayal, and even famous writers are surprised to discover that their publishers feel that way too. An agent, especially a good one, is of great value to an editor not because he handles a specific writer, but because he is the editor's best source of new talent. The famous writer who is now making very large sums of money thinks that he is now in a position more or less to dictate terms to his publisher—figuring that the publisher really needs him a lot more than he does some agent—and so is surprised when his publisher says that, no, he can't suddenly send all the checks directly to the author. It has happened many times that an author and agent fall out, and then the author wants the checks sent directly to him. The publisher frequently will agree, as long as the agent gets one check for his regular percentage and the author another for his. The author cannot get rid of his agent for any one book as long as a contract that the agent has arranged remains in force. The only time that an agent can be dropped by a writer is when he has a new book to take up.

The Author and His Editors

Assume, then, that either through an agent or from some other set of events a contract is offered for publication. Here the author should embark upon the establishment of the most important working partnership he may ever have outside marriage—and I know authors who consider their relationship with their editor as far more sacred than any marriage. It matters not at all what is written in any contract whether this partnership is a successful one or a trial and a hindrance. No lawyer can make people like and respect each other and decide to work in harmony—but if those bonds of mutual respect are established, it will be of the greatest benefit to everyone concerned. An editor will turn down a book sometimes because he has decided that he cannot work with an author, so if the relationship never gets established in the first place, no contract is forthcoming.

This lack of compatibility has happened to every editor and I can think of several times that it happened to me, although one example may be instructive. There was a well-known photographer and published author who wanted me to do his next book. He was a well established and highly regarded person and full of self-importance. When he brought me his book, which I very much wanted to publish, he arrived with not only the manuscript but also a set of instructions. He wanted to make all the basic publishing decisions—the design in detail, the method of printing, the exact printing plant where the book was to be made, and a host of other things that are normally the exclusive prerogative of the publisher, the one who is, after all, putting up the money. As a practical matter he wanted to be his own publisher while using our money, and since I didn't agree with him on a number of obvious points—he had, for one, designed a terrible jacket—I had to turn him down. He was surprised and outraged, as his sponsorship had been of the very strongest, but when I realized that I wouldn't have the normal control over what happened, I backed off.

The first thing for each side to remember in establishing the editor-author bond is that the text to be published is not sacred. The author should never refuse to listen to an editor's suggestions, and the editor should never fail to pay attention to an author's feelings. An author should remember that Ezra Pound edited T.S. Eliot, heavily at that, and so it is hard to think that any text comes perfect from its creator. It is also well to remember that an editor has commercial as well as literary interests in mind, and so his aims may not be exactly the same ones that animate the author. Writers, then, should listen to their editors and not be affronted by their suggestions. The editor is the author's representative inside the house and must be as bursting with enthusiasm as the author can make him, and if the editor feels that what he has done has improved what he is handling, everything works better.

In the matter of revisions, then, a professional author will listen carefully and try satisfying as many of his editor's concerns as he can. No book editor has the time to spend on extensive detailed revisions and changes, so what he will ask for will usually be that which involves only a small amount of time. The difference is in attitude. The amateur argues and protests and the professional listens and accommodates. When an editor knows that he is dealing with someone reasonable, the stage is set for a productive collaboration.

Titles

Take the matter of a title. Most manuscripts come to a publishing house with a title, and some authors are deeply wedded to it. The title of a book then often becomes the first matter that gets discussed between author and editor. It is here that a good editor will take the trouble to give his author a lecture—if needed—and the author will listen carefully if he cares for the success of his book. A novel can be called almost anything, and unless the title has

33

been used before or conjures up a repellent image or implies something the author hasn't thought of, an editor will usually leave it alone. Who, for example, would think that a book entitled *Song of the Wind*, which sounds sweet and innocent, is actually described in words such as "A fashion mogul can't stop loving the Nazi who destroyed her family"? Who would expect that *When the Bough Breaks* describes a book where "A double murder pitches a Los Angeles child psychologist into a web of evil"? What, after all, would you expect from a book called *The Sun Also Rises*? Any consideration of the titles of novels is likely to convince anyone that if it sounds reasonable it doesn't really matter what it is called. The editor's lecture should be reserved for nonfiction, because here matters are very different.

The basic rule is that for a book that is about something, the title should convey by itself what that something is. What authors forget is how often all that is known about a book is its title. In the announcement issue of *Publishers Weekly*, for example, many publishers merely list titles, authors, and publication date, sometimes with a category code—F = Fiction, NF = Nonfiction, M = Mystery, and so on—but that is all. In any number of other places, all that a searcher has to go on is a title. In the Books-in-Print listings as well as the subject guide, all that appears are title and author.

One would have to guess that the *Subject Guide to Books in Print* is among the most widely consulted reference books in publishing, and yet all it lists are titles and authors under the various headings. Publishers' backlist listings in their own catalogs, bibliographic references in other people's books, professors' reading lists, and who knows how many other places all are little more than title and author lists. How is anyone to know what a given book is about if its title does not announce it? That is the point to remember.

Some years ago I had as an author a very nice old man who had written a couple of successful historical books. He was a student of Shakespeare as well as an historian, and wrote a book that he thought plausibly filled in the gap in what we know about Shakespeare's youth. In the conventional biographies of the Bard, there is a considerable unknown period between his teens and when he showed up in London, at the age of twenty-four, seemingly fully formed and ready to establish his genius. My author thought he could make a good case for Shakespeare's whereabouts during that time and what he was doing, and as far as I was concerned, what my author said made sense. I knew that Shakespeare was of perennial interest, so I was willing to publish. The trouble arose when the author wanted to call his book *Like to the Lark*. It was a quote from his subject, of course, and sweet enough, but it didn't tell anyone what the book was about. He was willing to accept a subtitle *The Early Years of Shakespeare*, but really didn't want to give up his title. I tried to persuade him that it should be changed but I never could suggest one that seemed so much better that he was willing to give up his own. *Young Shakespeare*, *Shakespeare's Lost Years*, *The Making of Shakespeare's Genius*, and any number of variants on these all seemed to be wanting, and as my author was so enamored of his title, I eventually gave up. The book came out to little notice, perhaps due in part to the hostility of the academic establishment that resents outsiders trying to encroach on its territory, and it failed to establish itself as a backlist book, most probably because of an inappropriate title. Think only of a college student, say, trying to do a paper on Shakespeare. In searching out some books on the subject, will he or she be likely to find *Like to the Lark*?

Authors who have labored over every word of their book are usually unhappy with the idea that a title is so important. It serves not only to identify their book, but also to give it an emotional cast even if that shading is of the most sober and straightforward variety. The title is what draws people to the book or tells them that it may safely be ignored. The author remembers what he has written, but the prospective reader still doesn't have any taste of it, and so must start with all that is available, and that is the title. If a good book comes in to an editor with a title that is wrong for it, then his first task is to persuade the author that something better is needed, and it is the author's task to listen.

When a contract is signed, most publishers routinely send the author a publicity questionnaire. It is surprising how often authors misunderstand all this. Some will ignore the form, some answer the questions facetiously, and some provide a virtual biography. The fact is that a publishing house needs help from an author if it is to publish his book in an effective way. Authors should understand that the more information they provide, the more they will control what the publisher does and says about them. Book jackets usually have a short biographical note on the author. If he has provided them with a text of such a note, then he may see it used just as he sent it. If he had given the publisher scant information, then the publisher will have to write the note himself. Without guidance it may easily be in error.

What the writer would be well advised to do is provide his publisher with a draft of everything the latter is going to say about him and his book. The writer should provide a biographical note as well as a more extended treatment for background. He should provide both a short and long version of the flap copy, and a draft of catalog copy. If he has had any experience at such things, he can try his hand at a press release to be sent out either with the book or as a separate sheet. He must expect that none of these things will be used in a form even remotely close to what he sent them, but he should be aware that they will prevent factual errors from being made.

Then there is the matter of a photograph on the back of the jacket. If book buyers want to know about an author's background, they also want to visualize him as a real person. Theoretically this should make no difference, but it does. There is little doubt in publishing that the famous picture of Truman Capote on the couch that appeared on the back jacket of his first book, *Other Voices, Other Rooms*, made a great difference. Here was the young man languidly draped over a settee looking for all the world like . . . well, one certainly wanted to see what he had to say. Moreover, think only of how you conceive of Hemingway. If the words Ernest Hemingway do not at once bring into your mind Karsh's photograph of white-bearded Papa in a white turtleneck sweater, I would be surprised. Writers are somehow reluctant to understand how important photographs are, and have often resisted attempts to have a good photograph taken. Unaccountably, some publishers usually are not willing to pay for a picture of an author and frequently make do with a poor one. My view is that a good picture is an important part of the publisher's selling and advertising effort, and that a publisher should pay for one if the author doesn't have a good one already. I paid for the picture of Martin Gardner posed with the statue of Alice in Central Park that is on the back of *The Annotated Alice*, and have always felt it money

37

well spent. To gauge the importance of pictures, notice how often a photo of the author is included in the ads for his book.

After submitting a manuscript, the author's first responsibility, then, is to cooperate with his publisher in supplying what will be needed for the latter's selling efforts, and to work with his editor as the book needs. If these first important steps are taken with no trouble, then the author will next have to work with his copy editor, and here, as usual, a little understanding is a great help.

Copy Editors

To a publisher, it is absolutely amazing how many authors fail to understand what to expect from a copy editor and how to work with him or her. The copy editor's job, of course, is to protect the writer from mistakes. The writer should regard what the copy editor does with gratitude, for his or her only aim is to make the writer look as good as possible. He should be respectful, patient, and precise in all his dealings with his editor. The number of authors who are irritated by copy editors, brush off their queries, and can't be bothered to work with them only serves to demonstrate to publishers that many authors are in fact amateurs.

The proper relationship should be as from one professional to another, for anything less serves to put the book itself at risk. Authors sometimes seem to forget that if a reviewer catches an error, the blame is borne by the author, not the copy editor.

It should also be remembered that if an editor learns that an author is sloppy or unreliable or is giving the copy editor a hard time, then the editor's enthusiasm is likely to be dampened, and a book that loses its editor's positive feelings is going to wind up with less of a push from the publishing house itself. The author will never know that an ad, say, that could have been for his book was instead run for another one because his editor didn't push hard enough. When I was an advertising manager, we used to have meetings in order to allot extra money for ads to push the books that were going well, and how I would spend the money depended a lot on how everybody felt about each book. Sales figures were consulted, of course, but since no one had any special obligation to spend money in any given direction, where it went depended on how people felt about the different books. An author who was a terrible pain would get left out, and one who every-one thought was deserving would get something extra. The author who never got that kind of extra help never knew what he was missing, but he was missing it all the same.

Galleys

After he has finished with the copy editor, an author's next involvement with the publishing process is in read-ing, correcting and returning his galley proofs. Almost all type today is set by computer, but habits established for centuries do not change easily, so what an author gets are still called galleys. He is also expected to comply with the provisions in his contract that any changes that he makes in the galleys that exceed 10 percent of the original cost of composition will be charged to his account. It is amazing how many authors do not know the meaning of this provi-sion. As with so many other things, it is a leftover from the days of metal type, when each line of type was cast as a metal slug, and to make a change in a line, a typesetter lifted out and discarded that metal slug, set and cast a new one, and then inserted the new slug in the right place. If a couple of words were added to a line, then that line would become too long and so the next line down would have to be reset and perhaps even more lines until all the words would fit in and justify (i.e., the line would be even at the left and right margins). It was common for a few added words to require the resetting of a whole paragraph, and so corrections involved time-consuming and costly hand-work. The practical effect of the technology was that the cost of correction was high, and so what might seem to an author to be just a few corrections quite easily could reach more than 10 percent of the cost of composition. Careful authors and proofreaders would therefore read their galleys and mark changes and corrections that were required because the original setting contained an error, marking them *P.E.* in the margin, for Printer's Error, and thereby not be charged with the correction. Any other change was marked *A.A.* for Author's Alteration and would be included in the calculation as to whether or not the cost of correction totaled more than 10 percent of the original. Today it is as just as easy to run up a big corrections bill as it ever was. Just because typesetting has switched to computers doesn't make corrections any easier than they used to be. Each change still has to be found, carefully made, and checked.

Here we should note a practice that has caused a number of outraged exchanges between authors and publishers, which is that the author is usually not told what he will be charged for corrections at the time he makes them but finds the charge much later, in his first royalty statement. The reason for this is that the typesetter does not know how much time the changes will take until they are made—changes usually being billed at a per line rate—and cannot make up a bill until his changes have been seen and approved, for there may be errors even in his changes. Thus until revised galleys are okayed, he doesn't know what the proper charges come to. His bills will arrive some time after the work has been done, so no editor can call his author and tell him what may be the latter's cost until long after the work has gone to a stage where no more changes can be made. It is thus a near impossibility for an editor to warn an author as to how much of a charge he is going to have to stand. An experienced editor should be able to look at galleys and pretty much tell whether an author has done too much in the way of corrections and/or additions, but he can never put a number on it. Very few editors send out such warnings even when they could. The kind of author who makes a lot of changes is usually headstrong and insistent upon them and will frequently say that he doesn't care what they cost: they must be made. He will remind the editor of whose book it is and whose money is being spent, and the editor will shrug the matter off. This kind of author then often creates a row when he finds out the cost of the changes.

The way for an author to avoid all this and for an editor to keep things within normal limits is for the editor to make sure that the author has a professional attitude about his galleys. The changes that really need to be made should be, but to alter how he says something, or to try and change or improve an effect is the mark of a beginner. Even some well-known writers nonetheless can act as beginners.

When I was still very young, the Doubleday editorial department was all in one huge room, and the only separations between desks were chest-high movable partitions. I sat all the way at one end, but even though she was all the way at the far end, it was perfectly possible to hear every word spoken by Clara Classen when she called Kenneth Roberts in Maine. Clara had been Roberts's secretary when he had been a Doubleday editor himself and then had become his editor when he left to write his hugely successful novels. She was, it will be admitted, one of those people who thought that the louder you shouted into the phone the better your voice would be heard at the other end, but even so it demonstrated that everybody was working in a fishbowl. As a result, I later heard all the negotiations in which Ken McCormick was involved when he was offered a new book by William Saroyan. Ken was our highly esteemed editor in chief. It seemed that Saroyan, though very famous, had no loyalty to any publisher but only wanted as much money as he could get. As I remember it, the agent offered Ken a three-book deal in exchange for a very large *nonreturnable* advance. Guarantees were pretty much unheard of in those days, and a lot of money was involved, but in the end, some deal was worked out, and Doubleday eventually got to announce a "major new work" by Saroyan that fall. It was an item called *Rock Wagram*. The "w" was to be pronounced as "v," but that's about all I found out about it, for I never got to read it. The manuscript came in, was set in type, and then was returned by the author completely rewritten in galley stage. I did see the galleys, every one virtually unreadable, being completely covered with corrections and additions, and with sheets of new manuscript attached at the side by staples. The whole job had to be started over again, and the complete new setting cost more than the original because what we got was such a mess. The book, moreover, was in no way improved by the rewrite, was at once an expensive dud, and never earned enough to pay back the guarantee, let alone the two settings.

Besides the simple cost of corrections, there are deeper and more serious reasons for not tampering with galleys beyond correcting actual mistakes. It is in the form of uncorrected galleys that the publishing house sends out advance copies to book clubs, to early reviewers, and to people who the publishers hope will provide usable quotes about the book. Early reviews are particularly important in having the trade make an assessment of the importance of a book, so even though *Kirkus* and *Publishers Weekly* can hardly be called thorough or comprehensive because they are limited to such a short format, they carry great weight and set the tone for all the other review media. All newspapers must regard books as being in some sense part of the news, and any newspaper book review editor who is selecting what to include in the limited space allowed will readily admit that the perceived importance of a book is what makes him either assign it for review or let it slide. Importance and its perception can be established to some degree by the publisher promising to spend large sums of money on a book and making good on that promise in early announcements. If the publisher's promises are backed up by a good notice in *Kirkus* and elsewhere, then the book becomes established as something that should not be ignored. An aura is thus attached to a book long before it is even printed and sent out to the regular review lists.

At about this time, some comments will be coming back from the early readers, and the book club response will also come in. A few good quotes and a prospective book club deal give the publishing house outside confirmation of its own opinion, and the whole process of building up a big book is begun. Central to all this activity is the notion that the book being read is the same as the book that will shortly be published. If the author then decides to change a crucial opinion, delete a highly notable story, or add significant qualification to some strong statement, then the early readers will feel betrayed, and some of the things that they have already written may no longer be appropriate or even true. A writer should thus understand that he is by no means the only one who is reading his galleys. Others who are reading them are, in fact, the most important readers his book will get. At that point his book is already well into the publishing process and much that either will or will not happen to it subsequently has already been decided.

The conclusion an author should draw from all this is that the point at which he leaves his book occurs when he has satisfied all the copy editor's queries and the book is released for typesetting. From then on, the book is in a very real sense no longer his, and not within his control. That he gets to control his galleys should never induce him to lose sight of that basic truth.

Quotes

Since it is at the point where a book is in manuscript or uncorrected galleys that quotes are solicited, it is well that we pause to consider this much maligned publishing practice. It rests, of course, on the old established advertising practice of endorsements. The idea is that if someone I know, or know about, or think a lot of, says that something is terrific, then it really ought to be terrific. In my day, it was Johnny Weissmuller telling us to eat Wheaties, and in more recent times it has been Mary Lou Retton being enthusiastic about batteries, but whether it is cars or whisky or fountain pens, the people trying to sell them all feel that the implied integrity and disinterestedness of some well-known figure carries more weight than a mere anonymous exhortation. The brat who hears "Eat Wheaties!" is more than likely to respond, "Yeah, says who?" At that point, if the answer is, "Roger Clemens, that's who!" the command does seem to carry more conviction. Thus in the crass and cynical world of commercial hype, endorsements are the stock-in-trade of money-hungry agents and hard-boiled advertising pros cashing in on the hero worship of the young, the innocent, the impressionable. And, of course, all that is only too true. And even though the smart-ass brats we have today know perfectly well that Mary Lou is paid a bundle to go zowie over batteries, they still smile when they see her. What do you expect? Mary Lou is a terrific girl. Even if she does get paid, she is still a terrific girl.

In book publishing, of course, few are as grubby as they are out there on the sweaty socks circuit, and to prove it, nobody pays for endorsements. That is, they don't pay by handing people checks made out for dollar amounts, so the fiction is that all book endorsements are done for free—out of the pure motive of bringing to the fore unrecognized talent who might otherwise fail to achieve proper notice. It isn't paying off old personal debts, or in order to get a favor callable when you need an endorsement yourself for your next book, or for any reason such as furthering your own standing. Book quotes are done for love and for literature and for the public weal, and anyone who questions that just doesn't love the World of Letters. Publishing is different. It's clean. There's no overt quid pro quo. If someone says he likes a book, he really does like it. They are selling apples there, not oranges. You can count on it.

All these sour potshots at an easy target should, I suppose, illustrate the ambivalence that those of us who have had to deal in such matters feel about them. There is nothing wrong with an endorsement. Hemingway said some wonderful things in a letter to Malcolm Cowley about Beryl Markham's book *West with the Night*. He probably would not have let anyone use what he said while he was alive, but when a publisher wanted to reprint the book forty years after it first came out, they were able to quote his letter. It's good to see that the book is enjoying a revival and the recent paperback edition is approaching the multiple 100,000 mark. Now everybody is certain that Hemingway wasn't paid anything for what he said, and that is one big reason that people are sure that he meant it. One should take notice as well because he didn't say that kind of thing about every book—indeed he hardly ever said anything nice about any other book—so the rarity of his statement makes it all the more convincing. And that is why it is valuable to the author and to the publisher, and that is why the rare statement from any famous author is so sought after.

But if a rare statement from a famous author is so valuable, doesn't a famous author get besieged for them? Yes, he does, and that's where the problem arises. Famous Author hasn't had a hit for a while. He is in fact languishing. Publishers send him first novels. He reads them. He likes one and writes to the publisher saying something like "The most promising young novelist I have read in years . . ." and maybe makes a couple of other nice comments. They get used in a big ad campaign. Famous Author likes to see his name in print, established as an authority and all that. Famous Author gets more books, reads more, pretty soon thinks some new book is pretty good, and writes the publisher. Before anyone realizes what is going on, Famous Author seems to have given fulsome praise to quite a lot of people, so many, in fact, that his name on a quote begins to carry less weight, and advertising managers come to think of Famous Author's words as being on a par with Harold Stassen's political endorsements. What was once hard coin has become Continental paper. Famous Author stops getting books from publishers.

What, for example should we make of this? Writing in *The New York Review of Books* for June 26, 1986, Robert Towers says: *"Transactions in a Foreign Currency* arrives accompanied by a salvo from *The New Yorker*'s biggest guns—an excess of blurb that might well make a prospective reader wary. Actually, these tales from the Age of Cocaine turn out to be quite entertaining. The sensibility . . ."* He goes on to be quite positive about the book. The question, of course, is whether he would have bothered with the book in the first place if it had *not* been accompanied by a salvo of *New Yorker* names, no matter how slighting he is of the fact that the quotes are there. For a publisher and for his author, the consideration always has to be to get the book noticed to begin with, and so he uses the quotes if he can.

We will have a look at the literary game a little later, but for this consideration of a part of it, we should only note that the whole matter of quotes and endorsements is difficult. When done right, it can give a book a great boost, and when handled clumsily, it can tarnish the reputation of all concerned, and yet the only real difference is one of taste and style.

An author's position in the gathering of quotes should be the same as that of a candidate for a very choosy club—he should stand aside and let his sponsor do the promoting. He should affect surprise and delight at good comments and pretend to know nothing about what his publisher is up to. He will, of course, have had a talk with his editor about who to try to obtain quotes from, and what the writer's relationship is to each of them. They will have discussed which people would be more desirable to get something from, and his editor will then have modified that with what he knows from other sources. The galleys will then have gone to a pretty carefully selected bunch. Galleys are expensive, and sending out more than a few sets usually costs more money and time than it is worth, so, as when one solicits people to write supporting letters to an Admissions Committee, the list is not idly drawn up.

It is one of the finer points of etiquette that the author should write thank-you notes to those who have said nice things about his book and consented that they be used for publication. His stance is that since he did not himself solicit them they come as a happy surprise, and therefore the gratitude should sound as genuine as he can make it.

Once his galleys are returned to the publisher and his quotes are gathered, there is little for a writer to do until publication day. At that point, if his publisher isn't giving him a party, he ought to have a small celebration for himself. From then on, his book is public, and what happens, or, more often, what fails to happen, is not in his control. He must learn to bear whatever time brings.

Reviews

Some publishers occasionally give a party to mark a book's publication, and of course the author is expected not only to be there but to have rounded up all his literary or luminous friends as well. The theory has been that a big party would attract potential reviewers and the bookstore and newspaper people would want to get free booze and meet an author and the result would be more notice for the book. This has, to my knowledge, never happened, and I don't know why publishing parties are still held. My advice to both authors and publishers is not to spend money on a party on the expectation of getting public notice. If it is done to make everyone who is involved with the book feel good or to garner a certain kind of attention in the trade, then it may be worthwhile. What a writer should know is that a party has often been used by a publisher as an excuse for not spending some real money on space ads. If his invitation to a party comes along with an ad schedule, however, he should understand that his publisher really does think that his book is something special.

After publication, a writer then gets to read his reviews, and it is well if authors understand what reviews are all about.

If he is likely to feel that his entire ego structure has been put at risk when his publisher solicits quotes for his book, then the cohesion of his whole personality is called into account when it comes time for him to read his reviews. With publication, his book becomes fair game, and it is no longer shown carefully to selected, known friends. Anyone can read it. Total strangers in cities large and small are asked to write about it. No one feels any necessity to be nice. The author learns to his dismay that it is much easier and much more fun to write a nasty review than a good one. Nonetheless, some reviews are important, and some don't matter at all. The writer and his publisher must know the difference.

Generally speaking, the more commercial a book is, the less it needs reviews and the less they matter. If Taylor Caldwell, Jacqueline Susann or Judith Krantz depended on what reviewers thought of them, they would still be unknown, and both they and their publishers would be broke. Since it is the money from this kind of author that earns enough profit so that a publisher may indulge his literary pretensions by putting out the occasional volume of poetry, publishing houses rightly regard the literary crowd from a certain distance. These relationships have been quite constant over the years. Vulgar best-selling novelists are prized by publishers and scorned by the literary community. The darlings of the literary are scorned by the public and tolerated by the publishers. A few lucky authors bridge the gap.

Noncommercial authors need reviews. Simply because he is least well known, the least commercial author is, of course, the first novelist. Without notices, and good notices at that, his career will never get off the ground. With them, he may well go far. Generalizations about reviews can be unsafe. Nonetheless, it is obvious that good reviews help and bad ones hurt. It's just that each case is different.

Can good reviews sell a bad book? Probably not. Can good reviews sell a good book? Sometimes. Bruce Catton had absolutely rave reviews for two books and didn't become established with the public until his third. Then the same socko critical notices were heaped on it and his third book hit it big, bringing the first two back along with it. That is very unusual. What it does prove, though, is that even terrific reviews sometimes fail to move the public. It also demonstrates that durability is a great asset in a writer. Can terrible reviews kill a book? Yes, if it has literary pretentions. No, if it is strictly commercial. Is it better to be reviewed badly than not at all? Yes. Can anything be done about a bad review that was manifestly unfair? No. Even if a protest is published as a letter in a later issue of the rag, no one reads it. Should I as an author try and see to it that my friends get to review my book? Yes. Is this strictly ethical? No. Does everybody do it anyway? Yes. Who reads reviews anyway? Nobody has the slightest idea, except the group always includes all the people who are jealous of you. Should I as an author feel crushed when I read a lousy review of my book? No. Life is too short. Should I as an author feel wonderfully elated when I read a terrific rave of my book? No. Whoever wrote it will be sending you his galleys for a quote next month.

The whole business is complicated, perverse, and bears little relation to common sense, need, commerce or literature. I know of no one who is master of it. The most that can be said is that if you want to be amused, read the reviews that came out when some book that you know and love was first published. Until the judgment of history is available, however, writers and their publishers should only play the reviews game as best they can, remembering always that its outcome resembles a game of chance more than it does a serious reflection on the true value of their efforts. Writers should never write with an eye toward what reviewers will later say, and cannot change their book once it is published, so a sort of decent fatalism is their best emotional defense.

Promotion

If there is little that a writer can do about reviews of his book, there is much that he can do about its promotion. It is here that a writer most needs to remember that he is a part of the publication process, and that he can, if he will, make a great difference in how a book is known and received. One of a writer's most common misapprehensions is that his publisher is responsible for the promotion of his book. Rather, the most a publisher can do is help a writer out in his own promotion.

Here we must look at some history and consider some attitudes. I am old enough to remember hearing from people who had been in the book business in the twenties and thirties. In those days, the book business was small, snobbish and personal. There was no mass market for books. When radio came along, many book people felt that it would kill the book business. Who would take the time and trouble to get and read an expensive book when all he had to do was turn a knob and constant entertainment was available for free? Book people therefore predicted that radio would sharply limit book buying and that only serious and scholarly works would survive. As is so often the case, the hated rival had just the opposite effect. Radio opened up the book business and brought people into it. Radio talk programs about books were not only popular but closely followed. By the time I worked in a bookstore in 1949, radio programs were of supreme importance. Mary Margaret McBride had the greatest following, and we had to know in advance what she would be talking about every day and make certain the book was in because people would always ask for whatever book or author she talked about. The point that impressed me was that women would walk in every day around ten or eleven and say that they wanted the book that Mary Margaret had just been discussing. They didn't know what the title was or who had written it, they only had a vague notion that it had sounded interesting and that since Mary Margaret had been talking about it, it must be worth reading. That was the real point. It was not that they really wanted any given book, it was that they trusted Mary Margaret. It was also that they listened to the radio, and it was only because they listened to the radio that they knew about the book and had decided they wanted it. Radio had thus become a powerful selling tool for books, and not a rival at all. It was one of the engines that powered the great postwar expansion of the book business.

By the fifties, what had been said before about radio was then being said about television. TV was going to kill the book business. All the same fears were voiced again, and once more the true effect was the opposite of what the gloomy book people had warned against. TV opened up the great American mass market to books as nothing had ever done before, and it continues to do so today. Although people outside are not really aware of it, the book business has increased at least by an order of size in the last forty years—that is, as a whole it has multiplied by ten. This is due mainly to the growth of mass market paperbook publishing, but also to the establishment and growth of quality paperback publishing as well as the general expansion of the trade book business. The vast increase in the American book market may be the result of the huge increase in the number of people who have been to college, and one would have to think that this was one of its primary bases, but it is also due to the great general increase in the dissemination of all information brought about to a very large degree by television. It has already become commonplace to say that we are now living in the information age, but it is true, and one of the chief beneficiaries of that great social change has been the book business.

It may be that Mary Margaret McBride has been replaced by newscasters and talk-show hosts, but if radio had been replaced by television, it should be remembered that television has something like ten times the power that radio ever had. The audience may be diffuse but it is huge, and the great American mass may seem barely literate to the keepers of High Culture, but if that mass is ever turned on, the results can be awesome.

Now it is true that the beneficiaries of the power of TV are mostly books that can safely be called popular entertainments. TV is not much use in the promotion of high literary endeavor, or deep philosophical inquiry, so it is sneered at by people who think of themselves as the keepers of literature, but that is only as it should be. A mass audience hardly expects much else but tales of adventure, biographies of public personalities, and instructions for the expert preparation of food or the shedding of its consequences. Still, TV is very good indeed at what it does, and if an author had a book that would benefit from the exposure it can offer, he should pay attention and do what he can to make it happen.

Here we come up against attitudes. Some people are hungry for publicity and exposure and will urge their publisher's publicity departments to get them on programs when the book they have written is unsuitable for mass attention or they are themselves unprepossessing. These people should learn to be more professional. It is a waste to try promoting a book in a mass market if it simply doesn't have mass market potential. A good publicity director knows that trying to hustle the wrong book makes it a lot harder when he comes to hustle the right book. Authors who are eager should thus listen to their publicity director's advice and not push when push isn't needed.

More usually, authors don't like publicity and all that it entails. They think self-promotion is demeaning and that their work should speak for itself. They don't mind if their publisher wants to get quotes and spend money on ads, but they disdain the vapid and ill-informed approach that TV seems to imply. They feel that appearances, interviews, even autographing sessions are all a waste of time. They don't want to think that they have to sell themselves. They don't like appearances in public. There's the book. It ought to be enough.

Unfortunately, authors that feel this way are wrong. You do have to sell yourself. Your book can stand alone if it has to, but most things do better if they are sold, and you, the author, are your book's best salesman. Books are items of commerce offered for sale in public places. They are not sacred texts brought down from the mountain by gods and heroes. A book has been written by a person, and the person who may decide to buy it and read it has a much greater sense of identity with it if he feels he knows the author. The book therefore becomes the message between one person and another. No, anyone who wants his book to stand alone is doing neither the book nor himself justice. If it is his, he must not only stand by it, he must be willing to further its interests, for its interests are nothing but his own.

What this means in practical terms is that an author should consider that the time and trouble he is asked to take to promote his book is just part of his professional duty and should be fulfilled with as much humor and diligence as is needed. It is, in fact, the exceptional author who is asked to do very much. Most writers aren't that good-looking or that easy at public speaking and don't have the kind of book that lends itself to heavy promotion, so the little that most of them are asked to do should be done with all that much more grace. If a writer does a couple of autographing appearances at local bookstores, sits for an interview with a reporter from his local newspaper, agrees to attend a symposium organized by a nearby college, and makes a few speeches at women's clubs, that would be more or less par for the course. To refuse such mundane chores is to be churlish, but to seek them out is to deliberately waste time. The exceptions come up when a writer has a commercial book and is willing and able to go through the whole drill. In recent years, Judith Krantz has given us an example of this art form brought to its highest perfection.

Here are her comments on the subject from a letter she sent me in 1986:

I have strong opinions which I will write here in short form for you.

First of all, it is not only the writer who decides on a book tour. The publisher must be willing to pay for one and must have a publicity department capable of booking a tour. For a first-time writer, this is extremely difficult since everyone in the media would rather book a "name" than an unknown unless the unknown has a "hook," such as Anna Murdoch or Brooke Astor to mention a few recent novelists who got a great deal of press.

Secondly, the writer, of fiction or nonfiction (which is a thousand times easier to book since the "hook" is the subject matter), must be *able* to appear in front of the media. This is not easy. Many writers are too shy, many refuse to fly, many make a bad appearance and do themselves harm.

However, if these factors are overcome there is still the "hustle" problem. I remember well the first day of my first book tour, doing two radio interviews and coming home feeling as if I had talked about myself to a *shameful* amount and sure that I could never spend another such day. Now if the day doesn't contain at least eight to ten interviews, I don't consider that I've done a day's work. The difference is that I realize fully that promotion is nothing to be ashamed of and this took a certain amount of time.

My father was an advertising man and I had only to compare the budget of a book with the budget of any other product to realize that even a fat book budget will buy almost no space or time, certainly no television time at all. What I do is *assist* my publisher to advertise the existence of my books. I, in effect, am a town crier who performs a function: I announce that my new book is out and let the public decide if it wants to buy it. The only way to do this is to put myself on the line in body, willing to travel and ready to talk and answer the same questions over and over and over. Just this morning I spent an hour on the phone answering questions for an *internal* newsletter of a bookstore chain. Bookstores are of vital importance and bookstore contacts are essential. I've never met a bookseller I didn't like! They work for very little money and most of them must love what they do.

The would-be best-selling author must become as hardened as possible to the interviews that appear in the press. Few of them are exact. I don't think that more than five interviews in eight years, out of many hundreds of interviews, didn't contain gross errors in *quotes* of things I was supposed to have said. There is absolutely no point in writing to the editor; the editors always defend their writers, as I know from my days as a journalist. I approach each print interview with the certain knowledge that no matter how much I give to it, the journalist has come with his or her own point of view and will not be swayed from it. I prefer television and radio because you are heard saying what you said, not what the journalist would have liked you to say. But print is important to the sales of a book and book tours are about the sales of a book, not about the author's ego or dismay over misquotations. Doing a book tour is a way of working hand in hand with your publisher, whose margin of profit is not enormous to begin with. I feel authors *owe* it to them.

Self-promotion need not be quite so direct, and we will think about it more when we consider the literary game, but before we do, it is best to deal with one question that seems to come up over and over, and that is—if more money were spent, wouldn't my book sell better? It is common for authors who have made a big success in some field other than publishing to think that publishers are hopelessly backward in their advertising and promotion efforts. They are convinced that books are a commodity like anything else and that therefore any book would respond to a serious push. They usually have a book to promote and it is almost always about themselves, and when they discover that the publisher is planning to spend some small sum in advertising, a sum that to them seems so ridiculous as to be hardly noticeable, they sometimes offer to show the publisher how things ought to be done and volunteer to pay for a campaign themselves. This puts the publisher in an awkward position, for he knows that money spent like that is almost sure to be a complete waste, not to mention that by agreeing he is acquiescing to the author's judgment of his own incompetence. Nonetheless, the publisher invariably decides to take it, for in a way he cannot refuse, since anyone can run any ad that he can pay for. You or I, if we wished, could perfectly well take out an ad that said, Drink Moxie! or Vote for Stassen! and some old-timer might even wonder if you could still vote for Stassen, but most people would think of this as a waste of money. Korean entrepreneurs who take out full-page ads in *The New York Times* in favor of world peace do not seem to think they are wasting money, so who is to judge? If a publisher is confronted with an author who wants to spend money, he lets him spend money.

My first experience with this syndrome came when I was at Doubleday, and the man who has made his millions by selling Listerine had decided that he could sell his autobiography just as easily as he could sell mouthwash, and so was mounting a big ad campaign for himself. He was a bore, his book was a bore, and his ads reflected both. His book was a flop, money or no money. People like that always think the same thing, though, so a new example comes up regularly. We recently had a Wall Street tycoon decide to promote some drug he thought was the answer to everyone's prayer, and he spent vast sums on a book called *A Remarkable Drug Has Been Overlooked*. If anybody paid attention, I am not aware of it. What these people forget is that it has all been tried before, that it is based fundamentally on the idea that people will buy any damn thing if it is just promoted enough. But books aren't Listerine, or drugs, or anything else. Books are for reading, and if the reading is lousy, no amount of money can overcome that.

The Literary Life

But what can't be done with money, as any nice girl knows, can often be done with smiles. Here we enter the shallow waters of the literary life, a subject that as a longtime publisher I should in all likelihood eschew, although I won't. It should be emphasized, though, that my views on the subject are that of a publisher viewing the writer as a part of the publishing process. The question, of course, is whether the writer should make an effort to live the literary life and to try to achieve celebrity status by so doing. The answer, sadly, is yes.

If we have seen that a writer can and should make efforts to promote his book, then it is only a small extension of the same principle that he can and should promote himself as himself. We thus come almost at once to the writer as celebrity. And we are forced to admit that by making himself a celebrity, the writer increases his worth to his publisher, sells more of his books, and generally enhances his position in the literary world. It is the same as in our consideration of an author's photograph—if people feel that they somehow "know" a writer, they are more willing, even eager, to read what he has to say. One only has to think of the opposite case, when people may have heard of the name of a writer, but feel that *they don't know who he is*. For a long time this was the case of some highly regarded South American writers. Somehow they seemed to be just names, and because of that, no one particularly wanted to get their books. If, however, someone whom they have seen on the talk shows puts out a book, then people feel that they know him and so they buy his work. Anyone who has suddenly seen a familiar face on the street and realized that he was looking at someone he has seen on television is very likely to want to say hello to the person. The fact that the television person doesn't know at all the stranger on the street somehow fails to register until later, when the viewer thinks about it. It is the sense of familiarity that is the key. That is what makes for celebrity, and that is what translates into money. And that is why writers try making themselves into celebrities, and why their publishers willingly help their endeavor.

But if not everyone can be Norman Mailer, what can and should the average writer do to attempt to become at least a mini-celebrity? The answer is to think in terms of exposure. If an appearance or an interview or a speech results in good exposure, then make an effort to do it. Some writers feel that they are frittering their lives away at ladies' lunch parties, and so they may be if the exposure is too limited for the effort involved. Each writer has to decide whether the exposure costs too much in the way of time and effort or whether even a small gathering is worth the trouble. Keep in mind that a successful ladies' lunch can have results far beyond the circle of people who have been directly addressed, for ladies talk to other ladies, and a favorable impression can radiate amazingly far. Nonetheless, after a few dozen free lunches and lectures, a writer may turn down further opportunities, especially if they come to seem a chore. To those who do well at such things, feel elated by the attention, and please their audiences, these gatherings may serve as practice for larger forums and bigger platforms, until the TV camera seems only an extension of that eager, friendly face waiting for important answers. It all depends on just how much of a natural ham is in each writer. It also may depend on whether there is money in it.

When a writer gets to a certain point, people will offer money for his speeches, appearances or attention. Lots of writers do well on the lecture circuit, and it does wonderful things for their books. Anyone who is making big lectures and has a publisher who is organized well enough to see to it that his books are available at his lecture and at the local bookstores is going to sell quite a lot of those books. The numbers may not seem so wonderful at first, but they add up. Many writers actually make more from their lectures than from their royalties, so for those who are not too ground down by the life, lecturing is doubly rewarding. Any publisher, if asked by a writer whether he should go on the lecture circuit, will answer in the affirmative. Any writer who gets near all this should only remember that a good agent is a necessity, and that the lecture business is considered entirely different from that of publishing. It has its own practices and rules, and the promotion of books is strictly peripheral to the enterprise. For the author, however, it is the best kind of exposure.

It has long been the case that writers live in and come from the world of education. Books are the essential tool of the teacher, and the worlds of publishing and academia have been intertwined since before the invention of movable type. Today, an academic position is a secure base from which a writer can put forward his best work, and publication in turn serves to solidify his hold on his job. From the point of view of both the writer and the publisher, however, the publish-or-perish attitude of academic departments must be viewed with caution. Publishers can get used as the vehicles of advancement for ambitious academics and thus publish much that is marginal, while the professors themselves have on occasion become forced into constant petty self-promotion that is as enervating as it is demeaning. The academic world thus lives in an uneasy balance with the publishing world.

Authors would do well to keep in mind that publishers and editors tend to feel more comfortable with people who are writers first and foremost and who make their living from it. Those who are protected by an academic paycheck may indeed have freedom that a commercial writer does not, but the publisher knows that "experimental" books seldom sell well no matter what their reviews may have been. If the great freedom that academic safety confers on a writer is used to, so to speak, act out his fantasies, then the publisher is more than likely to regard this as mere self-indulgence. People in academia are well placed to play the literary game and thus tend to be better reviewed than their counterparts out in the commercial world, but big reviews cannot sell a book that people do not find readable. People simply will not read things because they think they ought to. I know, for example, that I ought to have read Proust, and I have indeed tried to do it several times, but I have never managed more than about forty pages. Poor Marcel lies in his grave without my understanding his longueurs or his passions, and yet, even at the potential cost of missing my Doctor of Humane Letters, I cannot read him. It is the same with some brilliant stylist who has had splendid notices on the front page of

The New York Times Book Review. I know that I indeed should read that book, and I also know that I won't. There is thus a whole literary genre that has grown up and flourished on academic security. Whether these works are read and whether they will last are somewhat problematical.

Lack of Ideas

One question that comes up all the time is, "What happens when I run out of ideas?" Every editor will sooner or later find himself with a writer who is in a very troubled state because he doesn't know what to do next. He has run out of projects. He feels he can't write, or that he somehow has a block. Many writers are enveloped by a sort of panic when they feel that they have nothing to work on. They need a goal, and without it a frightening void looms ahead. At that point they often ask their editor for an idea, an assignment, a lead.

My advice to both sides, writer and editor, is to stop. Unless, of course, one is a regular assignment writer, he should always choose his own subjects and write what he has decided to. If, at the moment, he has no interesting ideas and nothing to work on that seems important, then he should take a vacation and forget about writing. An editor, confronted with someone who may well be both a friend and the originator of the very things that make his job not just necessary but possible, often feels great pressure to supply his writer with an idea or a project. He may well give in to the pressure and find something for the writer to take up. Or he may do nothing more than go over the various things the writer has mentioned over the years, talking about the possibilities of each until the writer decides to pick up a long dormant idea or one on which he has always been too busy to work. By thus gently helping the writer to do what he may well have done for himself without help, the editor may feel that he has not interfered and not forced anything, but only done his job. My own feeling is that only if an editor steers a writer in a direction that he would find for himself anyway should the editor get involved at all. An editor, in my view, always invites disaster when he tries to direct an author, and an author who lets himself be directed is risking both his reputation and his livelihood. The underlying problem is the same one as in the case of a book written solely for money—the result will not carry conviction. A work created merely as something to do will always be weak, and weak exercises are seldom interesting to read. An editor should thus resist his first impulse to help, and politely but firmly draw back.

This advice must seem both unfeeling and impractical to anyone considering the plight of the writer or the long term needs of the editor, but I have arrived at my opinion from long observation and painful experience. A book takes a long time to write. It isn't like a magazine piece which can be knocked out in a matter of days or weeks and which, perfect or not, gets published and often forgotten. A book is something that will occupy a writer's mind for a year or so while he is working on it and then at least another year while it is being published, reviewed and sold. If it is something that has the quality of a chore, then the writing will display that sentiment whether the writer is aware of it or not. If the writer grows to be bored with or even to feel distaste for his subject, then that will show too. If an editor has suggested the book, then anything that goes wrong with it—from the trouble it took to write all the way to its poor reception—will be his fault. The writer will abjure responsibility for the book's fate if it is anything less than a huge success, and will of course claim all credit if all goes well. Any editor who suggests a book is thus put in a game in which he cannot win, no matter what the outcome, and those are the games at which it is best to be only a spectator.

But writers always say, how can I possibly not write? I have to pay the mortgage, send the kids to school, and most of all, be what I am. I have to write, for that is what defines me as a person. I can't afford to take a vacation financially or emotionally. Not write? My God, how could I live?

It is at this point that both writer and editor should call upon their professionalism. The writer should know enough to realize that he has to solve his own problems and that it is unfair to ask his editor to do for him what he should do for himself. The editor must take care to be friendly but at some distance, and must not fall into the emotional trap so invitingly opening up before him. The editor should remind himself that if William Faulkner cared enough about his writing to do it while holding down a job as a coal-stoker, then his writer friend probably isn't in as much of a bind as he thinks. The writer, if he cares more for the mortgage payment than he does his writing, probably should start thinking about joining an ad agency or a PR firm. There are plenty of writers who cared enough about the mortgage payment to earn a living at a conventional job and then write as well. William S. Baring-Gould had an entire career as a promotional copywriter at Time, Inc., and yet was able to put together one of the great triumphs of sustained and dedicated scholarship and produce *The Annotated Sherlock Holmes*. Other writers have simply acknowledged a fallow period and have done other things for a while until the ideas started to come back. Nothing is worse than for a writer to panic at the thought that he has no good new idea. It will start a self-reinforcing downward spiral that can, and often has, led to depression and alcoholism. An editor can often help a writer's emotional condition with sympathy and support, but the writer's best cure for a lack of ideas is to forget about writing and do something else. If it is money that is the problem, then he should get a job. Any job. Panic never got anybody anywhere.

Option Clauses

Many writers worry about how loyal they should feel toward their publisher and the question as to whether or not their option clause should be honored. Since there seems to be a good deal of confusion and misinformation surrounding the option clause, they should be sorted out.

Most publishers' contracts have a clause included that says, in effect, that the author's next book shall be submitted to the publisher and that only if the publisher and the author do not agree on a new contract will the latter be free to offer the book to some other house. Many authors feel that this clause binds them to their publisher forever, because each new contract has a similar one. This is not the case, and authors should understand a few simple points about option clauses before feeling trapped.

First, there is no such thing as agreeing to agree. An option clause either contains specific terms such as "upon terms the same as contained in this contract" or it says something to the effect that the terms are "to be agreed upon." If the terms are spelled out exactly, then it is not an option clause at all, but a contract itself for a second book. Thus the writer really has a two-book contract—usually on identical terms. So in that case the clause is not an option, but a contract. If the terms are "to be agreed upon," then it has no force of law and is merely an expression of intent. It is here that the trouble comes, because so many authors think that even if the clause has no legal standing, it has some sort of moral force and thus they feel obliged to honor it. The number of books that have gone to a publisher that the author didn't like because of this would amaze an outsider.

I have carefully explained the situation to any number of writers and still have seen them "fulfill the option" with their old publisher. In every case, this has meant that a reluctant author has published a book with a publisher who knows that the author will be leaving after this book. Naturally, the publisher not only fails to give the book any special effort, he usually turns it out in the most routine way possible. This guarantees that the unhappy author stays unhappy and offers another example of misguided and counterproductive ideas about loyalty. All authors should thus have firmly in mind that an option clause is meaningless. Even if they feel that it actually implies something, legal or not, they still should remind themselves that it mentions "terms to be arranged." All they have to do, if they don't like the publisher, is ask for terrific terms—something like an advance three times the amount of everything they made on the first book. The publisher refuses this, and the writer is thus not only free of any obligation, but claims the high moral ground as well. It is curious that some authors are so unwilling to involve themselves in the slightest controversy or argument that they will not even allow an agent to ask for better terms on a second contract than they got on the first. Such innocents sometimes survive anyway, but there is no reason for writers in general to be so put upon.

My strong advice for authors and publishers alike is to delete any option clause from all contracts. Any sophisticated publisher will know that an unenforceable clause is actually worthless and thus will not mind its deletion, and any author should feel better knowing that future relationships will depend on what happens to his first book. It is here that the question of loyalty, now divorced from legal entanglement, starts to become complicated. It would seem that loyalty should arise naturally from a good working relationship and a successful publication, and all publishers more or less operate on that assumption. In some cases that is indeed what happens, and a good author stays with his publisher as long as both sides are happy. Hemingway and Wolfe at Scribner's, Maugham and DuMaurier at Doubleday, Steinbeck at Viking, or Jimmy Baldwin at Dial, to name just a few, were all authors who got to a publisher and stayed there. In recent times this kind of relationship has been the exception, and it has become much more common for a successful author to follow the dollar and nothing else. It seems especially true that a change of publishers occurs after a big first book, although examples are perhaps not called for. The publishing business is just as competitive as any other one, and other publishers care nothing for the possible sense of loyalty that a young author may feel to the people who put him on the map. Offers are made to potentially money-making authors. Possibilities are discussed. Before he knows it, the writer has a new editor at a new publishing house.

Is all this good or bad, and if so, for whom? It seems to me that the most important consideration is that successful book publishing depends to some extent upon a good working relationship between a writer and his editor and publisher. If a writer feels comfortable with his editor, then I would advise him to be very careful before making changes, regardless of the apparent financial considerations. Naturally, if a writer is offered an incredible sum, he should probably take what he can get. If someone offers terms that are only marginally better than what he has, a certain conservatism will serve him well. He should remember that there are only so many good editors around. In recent years some authors have felt so acutely about this that their editor's role is written into the contracts and the departure of the editor from the company before the book is published is cause for the contract to become void. The contract is thus really with the editor and not with the publisher. Whether that is a good thing I shall leave to others to contemplate, but I know that when I signed a contract with an author, he knew that I would be his editor, so that was never one of my problems. I think that if I was so suspect that an author wanted to sign up with one of my editors rather than with me, then I would feel that something was seriously wrong with the way I was running my firm. It would seem to me that any manager of a large firm in the same circumstance should feel likewise.

Bad Publishing

It is truly depressing for someone who has spent a working lifetime in the publishing business to have to report that all too often the writer's question is, "What do I do when the publisher behaves unprofessionally?" That such a question is ever asked is an embarrassment; that such a question is asked all the time is a scandal. Nonetheless, it is true that unprofessional behavior is endemic in today's publishing houses. I found that out when I stopped being a publisher myself and agreed to act as agent for many of my old friends. I had, of course, never had much to do with working with other houses when I was a publisher, and so being an agent turned out to be a way to experience the actual working methods of the houses that signed my authors. What I found out, and what they suffered, was that practically none of the houses I dealt with were completely professional, and many of them were worse than amateurish. Writers, unfortunately, should understand that this is what they have to expect and learn to deal with it as best they can. One can only hope that by exposing the most common failings that a writer encounters, publishers will be encouraged to improve their methods and thereby polish their reputations rather than allow a patina of incompetence to accumulate.

There seem to be four general areas of difficulty that writers encounter, and we shall take them up in increasing order of reprehensibility, if such a term can be used. In any case, the first thing that will enrage a writer is sending off his book and then hearing nothing in return for a long period of time. The writer always wants to know how long he should wait before inquiring whether the publisher got the manuscript in the first place, and the general answer to that is one month. It should just be a query as to receipt, and not a request or a demand for a decision. The writer has to remember that unless the manuscript had been specifically solicited by the publisher or there was an overt understanding about sending it, it was sent to engage the pleasure of the publisher. The publisher did not ask for it and most likely did not know the manuscript existed until it was sent. He has no obligation to acknowledge it, read it, or do anything about it. The writer is in the position of a supplicant, and thus cannot make demands. Nonetheless, he can and must ask when too much time has passed.

From the point of view of the publisher, it is poor public relations to make an enemy of every writer who sends in an unsolicited manuscript, and it is worse to ignore a potential seller. Any well-run publishing house should look at everything that comes in, send back what is clearly not suitable within a matter of days, and acknowledge receipt for anything that looks as if it should be read by more than the first reader. All publishing houses must have first readers. I spent a year being first reader when I was at Doubleday, and later I was my own first reader when I had my own house. Thus, big or small if they are in the business, publishers must have someone who at least glances at what comes in and takes care of forwarding it or returning it. To fail to acknowledge receipt and to keep manuscripts for months without telling the sender anything is both very common and completely inexcusable. The only way a writer can deal with it is by sending polite notes from time to time and keeping his patience and his temper. It is useless to write nasty notes, but it is neither useless nor uncalled-for to ask for your manuscript back if you haven't heard anything for six weeks. Any publisher that has not reported back to a writer within this period is either incompetent or indecisive, and the writer should conclude that he probably wouldn't want to be published by such a slipshod outfit to begin with. The writer should send a short note to the effect that since he has not heard anything in x weeks, he can only conclude that the publisher has no interest in the manuscript and thus could it be returned. This will either get the manuscript back or it will bring a pained letter from an editor promising a decision shortly. Most writers are reluctant to badger publishers, thinking that if a manuscript is kept long enough it must mean that there is serious interest in it. Almost all failures of prompt acknowledgement are nothing more than sloppy management, and there is no reason for a writer to tolerate such things.

It should be pointed out that matters are very different

when a manuscript is sent to a publisher who already knows about it. In that case if nothing is heard back in two or three weeks, a query is in order. Only if a publisher specifically asks for time should it be given. Thus one of the things that an agent does do for a writer is to ask an editor about his possible interest in a book before sending it out, and then following up to get a reaction within a reasonable time. Just because a writer has published a book with a firm is no guarantee that a letter will be answered, a request followed up, or a new manuscript acknowledged promptly. Writers and agents must just keep track of what has been solicited by a publisher or an editor and what is pending, and write polite notes or call when things start to fall behind. Anger and sarcasm should be suppressed. Professionalism can and should be calmly insisted upon.

After dilatory reporting, the next most distressing thing that can happen to an author is for his publisher to lose his manuscript. It happens all too often in cases where the material is either difficult to replace or is in fact irreplaceable. The fault here, which seems to lie with the publisher, in fact lies with the writer. Publishers, even badly run publishers, do not set out to lose things. If they do so, the loss is usually due to some really unusual circumstance, often with shipping and mailing services. The United States Post Office lost two of my manuscripts over the years, but in the eyes of the writer, I was responsible because the manuscripts had been entrusted to me. No matter what I do, however, I cannot chase through the Post Office trying to find one manuscript box, and so if they cannot find it for me, I cannot find it for myself. If I have accepted responsibility, I am stuck with it. It is for this reason that publishers explicitly do not accept responsibility for the manuscripts that are sent to them, and thus a writer should never send out anything that he cannot replace. This is especially true for all illustrations, not to mention original artwork, and unfortunately, there are always writers and illustrators who forget this rule. In any case, the only insurance to cover a manuscript that is worth anything is another manuscript. In these days of easily-made copies that cost no more than the price of a lunch, any writer who sends out anything that he cannot afford to lose is worse than an amateur. If a manuscript is lost, it may mark the publisher as an incompetent, but it marks the writer as a fool. This is one case where the professional lapse by the publisher, real as it may be, is actually of small moment. The writer should protect himself to begin with.

The third problem that seems to come up all too often is when the writer must ask, "What can I do about bad editing?"

When it comes to obviously bad editing, an author must first consider whether the trouble stems from matters of substance. If it does, then his position is easily taken, and he should insist on it. When I was working as an agent, I had an author who had spent his life as a working scientist and had written a book about the current energy picture and its probable future. It had been accepted by an obscure regional publisher and a contract had been signed, and then the author discovered that an editor at the publishing house had decided to rewrite the whole book, putting it into "better" language. The editor had obviously had no scientific training or background, and thus had rewritten any number of sentences in such a way that the meaning had been significantly changed, and in every case had been turned into incorrect statements. The author was horrified to see that his book had become full of statements that were simply wrong. He asked me what to do, and after I learned that the editor actually did think that he had improved the text by what he had done—he said it was now "more readable"—all I could tell the author was to withdraw his book. He certainly couldn't let his name go on something that he knew was shot through with outright errors, and if the publishing house had an editor who didn't know any better, then the author was in a hopeless position. He did withdraw the book and later found another house willing to publish it as it was written.

This episode illustrates two things to authors. The first is that if a book is worth publishing at all, there are almost surely two publishers who will do it. Many authors erroneously feel that if they cannot get along with a given publisher that the alternative to publishing with him is to not publish at all. It may admittedly take a while to find another publisher if the first one goes sour, but to withdraw from a publisher is not to be condemned to silence. The second point is that in many cases the issue of who is right and who is wrong is pretty clear. If it is not, then the author must remember that it is his book, not the publisher's book, and that his opinion must prevail. The publisher, if he does not like the way things are going, can for his part refuse to publish, and this has happened any number of times. The author cannot force the publisher to publish against his wishes, and would be foolish to try, but neither can the publisher proceed against the author's wishes. Whatever the legal niceties, an author should remember that if he has sent back corrected galleys, he has at that point endorsed the wording of the text, and it is then too late to complain further.

The real difficulties arise when matters of style are at issue. I had a lady author whom I shared for years with another publishing house, a very distinguished and respected outfit that she had gotten along with perfectly well for the publishing of several books. She finally gave them her *magnum opus*, the culmination of a lifetime of work and learning and in my view a very important book. They gave it to a young editor who then proceeded to change the basic form of the hundreds of entries that made up the book as a whole, and soon the author had on her hands a manuscript with its hundreds of pages marked up in a way that she did not like and felt she could not accept. What to do? Were the changes a matter of substance? Well, not really. The information was not made incorrect by the changes, it was just put in a different form. The form, to be sure, was one that the author did not like, but she could not maintain that it was a distortion, only that it was in a style that was unconventional and, she thought, somewhat misleading. Since she was an experienced and valuable author to the firm, she took her problem to the president of the company, a man she had known for years. He was of little help, pointing out that to change her book back to the form that she had started with would be expensive, time-consuming, and would give him a problem with his own employees. He could not see that the difference that distressed her was of any great consequence, and tried to get her to accept the changes that his editor had made. There was at that point nothing for her to do but make a choice between accepting what had been done or withdrawing the book completely. She withdrew the book, ending a relationship that had lasted over twenty-five years.

There is, in my view, only one way to manage this kind of thing, and that is to never let it get to the point where a serious confrontation must arise. This means that an author should work closely with his editor and know what the editor is doing from the start. If extensive editing, rewriting or major alterations are warranted, then the author should ask for and get a sample of the first few pages before taking a stand. If the sample is good, then there will be no problem later. Any difficulty that does arise must be addressed at once and settled before it becomes compounded. Here a writer's sense of style, his standing and his eloquence at persuasion all will come into play. No matter what else, however, he must insist that everything stop until whatever controversy there is stands resolved to the satisfaction of both editor and writer. If he lets matters slide with nothing but a grumble, then he has no right to complain later. Only if he pounces on what he doesn't like as soon as he knows of it will his position stay secure.

A writer should remember that in any controversy over matters of style that come up between him and his editor, he has two powerful tools that he can bring into play. The first is the strength of his arguments, and the second is his ability to go over the editor's head.

If it comes to an argument with an editor, a writer should keep in mind the following. He should ask whether the changes are made because of some house policy. If the answer is yes, then the editor is almost certainly lying, since in all my years in the business I have never heard of any house having an editorial policy other than in strict copy-editing matters. The author can also ask whether a change is made in order to increase the books saleability. If the answer here, too, is yes, the editor is fishing, because he can never show a relationship between some small editorial matter and a book's acceptance, let alone a direct relationship to sales that haven't been made yet. If the editor maintains that a change will improve a book's chances to be well reviewed, or avoid bad reviews, then that is a real consideration, and an author should ask just how that would work. If an editor can point to solid cases where reviews were influenced by how a thing was done, then an author must listen. If an editor maintains that his proposed change is asked for in order to preserve the firm's standards and reputation, then an author should find out just how that works as well. Altogether, all discussions should be kept as friendly and as professional as possible, and emotional positions and attitudes must be suppressed. Many writers have found that their sessions with their editors, sessions that are supposedly only for the improvement of the book, have instead turned out to be emotionally distressing and infuriating when they are not depressing. If things get too bad, then authors must consider their ultimate appeal, which is going over the editor's head.

A writer has to remember once again that he is a part of the whole publishing process, and if he considers making an appeal to a higher authority, he is at that point doing something both political and dangerous. An editor who has a writer appeal over some controversy to someone higher up in the organization has at once a black mark registered against him. Editors in chief are not pleased when they find that they have to adjudicate a matter arising from the lower ranks, and presidents are even less amused. This could affect not only an editor's career and advancement but a writer's reputation as well if he turns out to be wrong. "Difficult" authors become well known, and troublemakers are not welcome anywhere. Thus if a writer feels that matters are so bad that he must make an appeal of his editor's position, he must remember that the outcome can only result in a blotch on the reputation of one party or the other. If it is a trivial matter that the writer is seen to be overfussy about, then the mark will stand against him. If he is wrong to begin with, the mark will be more prominent. He should only consider such action if the matter is truly serious and he feels absolutely secure in his position. In any case, what matters is good judgment. An author confronted with bad editors can only keep calm, do what he can, and in the end insist that what is being published is his book, with his name on it, and he therefore must stand as the final arbiter of what is said and how it is said. Anything else takes his book away from him, and he did not enter into a contract with the publisher to let that happen.

So far, all the unprofessional things that a writer can run into have been those in which he is involved and are matters that he can know about and have a say in settling. The ultimate and the worst thing that can happen to an author is for the publisher to make basic publishing mistakes about which the writer can do nothing. Here the best way to make the matter clear is to take an example.

Not long ago, as an agent, I placed a mathematical recreational book with a large and famous publishing house, one of the top dozen that now dominate the business. The editor who took it then handed it to a young man in her department to take care of, and I heard little about it until I got copies of the book and learned of its publication. It was not a success. It had a few very good reviews in specialty journals but no great sale. When I saw the book, I realized that it would be a disaster—one entirely engineered by the publisher. There was nothing to do but analyze why. After some thought, I came to see what the reasons were for this particular mess. The trouble, it seemed, stemmed from the circumstance that the publisher had completely mistaken the market for this book. Mathematical recreational books are a small but definite specialty within the business. Anyone who knows anything about them is aware that the devotees of such things are scattered widely and can be most conveniently described as being the readers of Martin Gardner's column on the subject in *Scientific American*. (This was when Martin was still writing it). The readership of this magazine is one of the most analyzed of any and can be most easily described as people with scientific training and often in scientifically related jobs who like to read about developments in fields other than their own. Thus they are scattered, well educated, financially secure, and mostly middle-aged. What the publishing house did was assume that the market for a recreational book was mostly a college campus one, that is, students. It is true that colleges hold many enthusiasts for mathematical games, but they are mostly in the faculty. The students don't have the time or inclination to indulge in such games, and it is a great mistake to target them as a market for this book. This, however, is just what the publisher must have done, for all the decisions that were later made were based on such an assumption.

To begin with, the format of the book was never in question. It had to be a large book because it would have problems in it that the reader could work out for himself. Its drawings and diagrams required a large size, so even as it was submitted at first, it was clear that the book would have to be 8½″ × 11″. Everything else was decided by the publisher. What did they do? In the first place, and most disastrously, a decision was made to publish the book only in paperback. This would be consistent with the assumption that the market was mostly college kids. Paperbacks are cheaper than hardcover, students are used to buying them, and softcover is most appropriate for a book that may be marked up and annotated by the reader.

Secondly, the book itself was made very badly, once again on the wrong assumption. The paper for the book should have been white, firm, crisp, and solid. Instead, in

79

order to save money and offer the book at what the sales-people thought was a suitably attractive low price, the paper quality was drastically lowered and was the cheapest possible, being buff color, rough textured, and with a notable print-through from the other side. Few would use it for working out problems, even if they had the time before the acid in the wood pulp turned the leaves yellow, and they then became brittle and fell apart.

In looking at the front jacket of the book, one saw a pastel, vaguely oriental, and busy series of unrecognizable symbols that were neither attractive nor comprehensible. The jacket was thus quite inappropriate, for what it should have been was clean and crisp, with an obvious example of what is inside showing openly on the cover. A potential buyer should at least have been able to make out what the book was about by glancing at the cover—and a good cover would do that—but this one didn't.

Finally, backing up their assumption, the publisher loaded this book into the college stores. I saw stacks of it in two college stores myself. Of course, the sale was modest, even at the remarkably low price that the publisher had been able to achieve, and the authors subsequent royalty statements confirm that a lot of them came back.

What can an author do about things like this? The answer, unfortunately, is nothing. It is the core of the publisher's responsibility to publish books in such styles and format as he deems best suited for the market. If he is wrong, it is his money that is lost. In this case, he could perhaps have asked someone experienced in similar books for advice—but most publishers choose not to do that. Afterward, faced with trying to learn from such a series of mistakes, an agent and an author can only protect themselves by trying to find publishers that have done well with similar books, and who seem to know what they are doing with a book of the type at hand. Even first novelists will study the publishers' performances and discover that some put out similar books far better than others. The writer, then, can only do the best he can with things within his control, and should remember that the writer is only one of a large number of people who all work and cooperate to get books out to the public.

A writer's place in the publishing world, then, is as the indispensable originator of the messages that are brought out to his audience. No matter how lonely, how solitary, how private is the act of writing, it is meaningless unless it stands as a communication, a message to be read. No writer really writes to consign his work to a closet forever, for even diarists expect that what is written will be read, even if only by themselves later, as a reminder, as a picture of what the person he once was thought at the time. All writing is for reading, and the whole publishing process is to make as many connections between writer and reader as is possible. Some writers long for huge audiences and fame and money. Others crave the respect of their peers or influence over the ideas of the important and powerful. Some write for their own pleasure, trusting that what delights them will strike others the same way. The motives are as varied as what each produces, but no matter what the motives are, each will wish to see his words in print, available to all. That is why a writer enters the publishing process itself, and not only what he writes to begin with, but what he does for it afterward will make a difference to the size and importance of his audience. He may feel at times that he is alone, but when the connection is made and his readers respond to what he has said, then his words live, and he knows that he has made something with a life of its own.

2

Editors in the Middle

Introduction

ON THE SURFACE, it would seem that a book publisher's editor has an impossible job. He is asked to be the pivot point in the publishing process and to possess diverse skills that can rarely if ever exist within one person. He must have native tact and an innate sense of diplomacy, for he represents the wants and needs of an author to the people within his publishing house, and he also represents the wants and needs of the publishing house to not only the author but also the outside world in general and the book trade in particular. The interests of these two sides are almost always in conflict, sometimes deeply so, and so he must make hard decisions, implement them firmly, and do what he can to reconcile them and to fulfill his own goal of finding, producing and marketing successful books.

What an editor does all day and why he does it is usually a mystery to an author and just as much of a mystery to most of the people inside a publishing house. Other people know that he is necessary, but do not really know why, and so he is likely to find himself regarded

82

with both tolerance and suspicion, but almost never with sympathy. Moneymen regard editors as unbusinesslike and given to allowing their emotions to rule their good sense. Those in the publishing company who do not have to deal with the public but who have other jobs regard the editor with a mixture of envy and contempt. The editor, after all, does go out to lunch on the expense account, does meet some people who are well known or glamorous, and does make important decisions, and that excites envy. But he seldom if ever has any detailed knowledge of the insider's competence in, say, production or art or sales, and that breeds disdain. The editor thus is often seen by insiders as a pleasant flimflam artist without any professional standing. The author and the agent often think of an editor as overly preoccupied with inside needs—he seems always to be in meetings—while he is insensitive to the author's concerns and too harried by the press of other work to pay enough attention to details. The inside people think of an editor as forever distracted and unwilling to give proper attention to their needs and sometimes barely competent to even make the small decisions required.

Being a book editor would thus seem to be a thankless, ill-defined job, the requirements of which would call for someone with an incredible education, a vast fund of sophistication, a thorough and detailed knowledge of all the jobs in publishing, a firm and sure ability to make prompt and accurate decisions, great power of persuasion, an unfailingly sure judgment as to what the public wants and will buy, and most importantly, an innate charm that naturally carries with him anyone he meets. Such a person, of course, does not exist, and an amazing number of people want to be book editors, so the truth has to lie somewhere else.

The book editor's job is, in fact, by far the most interesting one in publishing. It is as varied as it is surprising, requires creative solutions to a wide assortment of problems, and is enormously satisfying when it works as it should. In this section we shall look in some detail into what an editor really does do all day, and by so doing illustrate by example what is hard to define in general terms. The various sections that follow, when taken together, should provide a picture that explains who and what an editor is. No two are exactly alike, any more than two books are, so each person provides his own definition of what an editor is. It is therefore necessary to look at editors one by one, and as we meet each one, increase our understanding of what he or she does.

Kinds of Editors

The various editors may be classified according to the limits of their ability to make decisions—that is, the level of their responsibility—and rather than go from the bottom up we shall start at the top and proceed down.

At the top of the positions an editor can hold is the one of unlimited responsibility. This permits an editor to commit his house to the limit of the firm's financial capability, and he can do so without consulting anyone or needing any agreement from any other person. This is the position of the editor-owner, someone who owns the shares, or controls them, and can do what he likes. It is the position of the small entrepreneur who can and does simply go ahead and publish on his own. It may seem that in the real world this is merely a theoretical position to be in, but such is not the case. There are hundreds of small publishing companies turning out a few books a year that are simply run by one person or a couple. Some publish only

one book. Others publish in a highly restricted category—
say American antiques and nothing else. A number of
them are run as hobbies. Many are adjuncts to some other
enterprise, religious, charitable, educational or political.
Some grow in time to form a larger company.

Here, for example, are the comments of Walter Ken-
drick in an assessment of *The Pushcart Prize X* in *The New
York Times Book Review* for November 24, 1985:

> One's strongest impression while surveying this hefty col-
> lection is of the vibrant, indeed almost frantic vitality of
> noncommercial publishing. The presses and journals repre-
> sented here may be "small," but they make up for size in
> number: some 450 publishing enterprises made or received
> nominations for this 1985–86 edition, and in addition to the
> 55 pieces printed here, more than 200 others are listed in an
> appendix as "outstanding." Though the world of commer-
> cial publishing may increasingly resemble a shopping mall,
> packed with indistinguishable fast-read outlets, there is no
> scarcity of alternatives for those writers (and readers) who
> seek variety and a different kind of profit.

There are, in fact, over 12,000 publishers listed in Bowker's *Books in Print*, so it is not at all fanciful to note that
there are some thousands of editors who publish without
benefit of any consultation unless requested. To those
wanting to learn about publishing, this group may seem to
be an uninteresting or trivial example, since what is really
interesting and important is what goes on in the large and
established companies that are in business to make
money. To think this would be a mistake, however, because all editors on the way up, whether they realize it or
not, are groping for that ultimate position—to be able to
publish exactly what they want exactly as they want to do
it. The nearest anyone ever gets to that in a large company

is becoming editor in chief with a stated budget that can be allocated anywhere one wants, or else to have one's own imprint within a large unit such that one may publish within only very general budgetary constraints. The difference between the little operator who has a garage full of books and does his selling strictly by mail order, and the editor of a large company who has a huge organization that sells what he publishes is, of course, the size and weight of the organization.

Over the last generation, the distribution of books has become more and more concentrated, and now the general book trade is dominated by about a dozen very large organizations. The middle-sized companies that used to be able to exist have increasingly been squeezed out, and distribution has become effective only if done very big or very small. Thus very small publishers are highly specialized and very big publishers are both obsessed with and dominated by books that are, potentially at least, best sellers. These trends have been generally evident for at least the last thirty years and there is no reason to think their course will change.

What this does mean for editors is that the goal of an editor with a vast selling network at hand will be quite different from one with a specialty market. The size of their gambles and the rewards of their success will also be very different. At this point, therefore, noting his existence but also noticing his lack of impact on the larger scene, we shall leave the independent operator and consider the position of the editor in chief of an established house or the publisher of an imprint attached to a large house.

A top editor or imprint manager will have worked up to that position by having had a great deal of experience and an equal amount of demonstrated success. The routes up are varied, and we shall consider them later, but no publisher is going to let his company's most visible department be run by anyone who is not secure in his reputation for probity, knowledge and sound judgment. The days of the publisher-editor like Alfred Knopf, George Palmer Putnam or Rupert Hart-Davis are pretty well over, and in most houses the publisher and the editor are two different people. The publisher is what I call the moneyman, and we will devote an entire section to him later, so for now we must consider his editor, who in a big company holds a title such as editor in chief. Titles vary, and in looking at any given company, one has to be a bit wary before knowing what title signifies what responsibility. For our purposes here, the editor in chief is the man who decides what will be published and who makes the deals for the contracts under which the books are published. He must approve of all contracts that are signed in his department, and will have the power to hire and fire the rest of the people there.

Here we must make a brief digression into organizational theory. In any business organization, as in any large acting formal group, whether it be an army, a religious organization, a university or a government, there are two fundamental functions, and these are called line and staff. Line is decision making and acting while staff is advisory only. The distinctions are clear and explicit in an army, where there are line officers and staff officers, but in a business organization the distinction is no less important even if it is less explicit. The editor in chief has line responsibility and his advisors have staff responsibility. If a junior editor convinces his department to pay a huge sum to acquire a given book which is then duly published and turns out to be a dud, the responsibility lies with the editor in chief who was persuaded by his subordinate and not simply with the junior himself. The junior is expected to be inexperienced, to be given to misplaced enthusiasm, or perhaps to be swayed by the passions of the moment. His boss should know better, and even though he has the power to demote, move sideways, or fire the junior, nonetheless he will be held responsible by the rest of the firm for the young man's actions.

To find line responsibility in any business organization, one need only identify those people who are directly responsible either for hiring and firing or for getting money or spending it. The lowest functionary in a production department, if he has the power to let a contract to buy paper, have printing done, or even order the details of a shipment, has a line job. He can specifically commit the company and his signature on a purchase order is binding upon the firm as a whole, so he is line. Similarly, anyone who directly earns money for the firm is line. Salesmen, ad managers who place coupon ads, sellers of subsidiary rights, or anyone who actually gets money for the firm is line. Publicity, art, and all editorial and housekeeping functions are staff. It may seem that the distinction does not really matter, since all the various jobs are needed to acquire books, and produce them and market them, so all are equally important. Unfortunately, it does matter, because moneymen regard people who fulfill staff jobs as more or less interchangeable, and therefore they are paid far less well than those who hold line jobs.

While this is the formal position or organization in an editorial department, in practice it is much looser, and experienced senior editors do pretty much as they think best. As long as they have the confidence of the editor in chief, they often do actually operate almost without formal constraint. Outside of their own secretary and assistant, they cannot hire and fire, and with the editor in chief himself they must attend the weekly editorial department meeting and have their author deals ratified by its members, but it is very unusual indeed for a senior person to have a deal altered or turned down in an open meeting. We will look at meetings in more detail later, but for now it is only important to note that, in theory at least, a staff person *suggests* that a course of action be taken and then a line person *decides* to do it. Decision making in an editorial department can be a subtle and difficult matter indeed, and as we examine the various aspects of what editors do and who does what, the process may become more clear. The theory is only offered as a framework for a better understanding of the actuality.

The editor in chief or anyone else who enjoys his complete confidence is thus the most important decision maker in the company, because he commits a course of action for the firm as a whole when he sets in motion the process of publishing a book. No one—or hardly anyone—will come up to an editor in chief and say, "Why in God's name are we publishing that turkey?" The editor has his reasons, which usually make sense if you know them. All sorts of books are published for "other reasons." That is, everyone knows that they would not ordinarily be published, but in this case there are mitigating circumstances.

Taylor Caldwell, a popular and successful author who had been wrangled away from her previously perfectly competent publisher by an appeal to her sense of greed—a tactic that almost always works—had duly produced a best-seller every year or so. Everyone was happy until she sent in a thoroughly nasty, whining, self-serving and repulsive book about the cost of producing a best-seller, that is, *her* cost. In it she complained about everything from the monstrosity of the income tax law to the cost of her researchers to the slovenly nature of the maid, and threw in for extra comments about the reluctance of her editor to follow her specific directions, the lack of education demonstrated by her copy editor, and the indifference of the art department to her favorite color scheme on the jacket. It was, of course, a book that would only draw a laugh from a first reader and go back to the author in the next mail if its author were not known. In this case, it posed the question of whether or not the house wanted to go on publishing Miss Taylor Caldwell. If the publisher turned it down, she would certainly go away in a huff, and there was no lack of other houses to which her agent at once could go. If the publisher, on the other hand, wanted to keep her, he would have to swallow the book, and do the best he could with it. If greed will usually win an author, it will always win a publisher. A few simple sums demonstrated that the money lost on a small edition of her complaints, even assuming that no copies at all were sold, would be covered ten times over by the profits on her next best seller. Thus we were treated to the disheartening spectacle of a highly respected editor in chief of a major publishing house attempting to present an offensive book as if it were a worthwhile, interesting and important commentary on publishing practices—positions he did not believe any more than we did.

This is an example of the truth that in publishing it is usually easier to say yes than to say no. Senior editors know quite well that a great many books sink without a trace, but they also know that they have to keep putting out a list and also that they can never be sure what might suddenly take off. To balance the humiliation of saying yes to Taylor Caldwell, it should be noted that this same editor said yes to Jean Kerr when no one else would. Jean

Kerr, the wife of Walter Kerr, the prominent theatre critic, had been publishing pleasant little pieces about suburban life in various women's magazines, and every editor in New York had taken her to splendid lunches at superb restaurants and courted her for the novel that it was rumored she was working on, telling her of his willingness to go very high indeed to get it. She had turned each down, and then Ken McCormick, who was Doubleday's editor in chief, took her to *his* favorite restaurant. She similarly turned him down on a contract for a novel as she had everyone else, but Ken was persistent, and she finally admitted that what she really wanted was to have all her short pieces published in one volume so her friends could have them in one package. After all, no one kept old copies of magazines, and it would just be nice to be able to give her friends something in hard covers that would last a while. If he would do that, then he would get an option on a novel. Ken, of course, went for it, and signed her up. Inside the house, the book was presented for just what it was, a favor for a friend, and, in effect, a down payment on a novel contract. It was assumed that she would have quite a few friends of her own, so a standard first novel printing was ordered—it was 3,500 in those days—and in the hope that her friends were well-heeled, the price put on the book was artificially high—$5.00 instead of $4.00. That is a twenty-five percent increase and at today's figures it would mean a $17.95 book becoming a $22.50 book. It should be remembered that if a serious novel stands as a classic of something offered for sale for which there is a highly elastic demand, then light humor has a demand at least five times more elastic. In any case, the book was, of course, *Please Don't Eat the Daisies*, and it was not only the smash best-seller of that season, it was also a winner in

Hollywood. The extra dollar on the price produced pure profit, and the whole performance fully justified Ken's reputation as the best in the business.

These examples are both illustrations of why it is sometimes easier to say yes than to say no—a subject to which we shall return in considering young editors. They also are demonstrations of decisions that only an editor-in-chief can make. Only the most senior and the most trusted decision maker can be allowed to make judgments that do not seem on their face even slightly sensible. In these examples the decision was undoubtedly right, but the sad truth is that seemingly bad decisions are all too often just that—bad decisions. You need only ask the man who decided to pay a million dollars for an unwritten novel by James Jones and wound up getting for his money a novel called *Go to the Widowmaker*—widely felt then and now to be the great man's weakest work, as well as nonstarter in the best-seller race.

The editor in chief of a publishing house of any size is thus a very busy man. He must be aware of what is going on in his own department and approve or modify or disapprove of what his colleagues and subordinates are doing. He must meet with and make joint decisions with his art department, production department, and most especially his sales, advertising and promotion departments. He will be in almost daily contact with his rights manager. He must regularly meet with the publisher and representatives of the owners whether they be actual owners or securities analysts. Any truly significant corporate decision—to start or stop a new division, to enter or drop a different sort of business, to merge with another company or anything else that will make a fundamental change should be something of which he is aware and has a hand in. Some companies exclude their top editor from such matters, but they do so at their own peril, for he is not only far less insulated from the outside world than business managers are but also much more likely than the average corporate manager to have a sense of the times and where they are drifting. He must, of course, constantly monitor the performance of his subordinates, and he must handle his own authors. Big-time money-making authors and agents do not want to deal with anyone but the headman, and they are right to insist on talking to him directly. And in case this is not enough to do in a day, he must talk on the telephone a lot, and he must read. His desk will be piled high every day with correspondence, internal memos, reader's reports, pertinent clippings and, of course, manuscripts.

Anyone who can do all the things that are required of an editor in chief will be well paid and at the top of his profession. In New York there are a few of them, but because the ideal picture we have drawn is so hard to fill in practice, their jobs have been broken up into more manageable pieces and there are people who act as editor in chief of a small portion of the list the house publishes. In a textbook house, this situation is both natural and usual. An editor covers a given field and often only deals with the publisher, and some scholarly houses do not even have an overall editor who is expected to cover the whole range of what the firm does. In a trade house, there are the heads of special kinds of books, and while different houses have different systems, the following categories will usually have an editor who handles these books exclusively and reports only to the editor in chief—mysteries, westerns, cook books, children's books (usually a whole department), science, backlist staple books, religious books, and dozens of others. *Literary Market Place* (*LMP*) lists over seventy categories, of which one is fiction and one is general nonfiction. This is not to say that when I was handling a list of western fiction I could not handle a novel or a general book. I could and did, but no one else could or would handle a western.

Editors with literary, artistic or intellectual pretentions tend to look upon western novels as strictly the lowest totem on the editorial pole, but when I was editing them, we had a president in the White House who not only read westerns, it was widely rumored that they were *all* he read. It came out later that he was dyslexic and was accustomed to having important information come in through oral briefing, but we thought his reading material only demonstrated his intellectual incompetence. Forty years later, his performance does not seem so bad after all, and now that we have recently had a president who read westerns, we can only hope that in another forty years historians of our period will be equally kind. Ike read Luke Short and Ron read Louis L'Amour, but one doubts whether anyone ever suggested that Eisenhower give Luke Short a medal.

In any case, the lowly western is an illustration of some very important things that editors should understand. In the first place, they demonstrate—although no more than all books do—that a publishing house actually is nothing but its contracts, and the rights that flow from these contracts. In the thirties, Doubleday had published some very second-rate westerns that featured a character called Hopalong Cassidy. Then television came along. It turned out that the original contracts for these books contained a television clause even though at the time they were signed there was no commercial television, let alone a practical device for its dissemination. Nonetheless, the legal language was good, and so when Hopalong became a big thing with the kids on television in the fifties, Doubleday reaped some very large sums in rights money. At the time, it had not yet been established that an author or publisher could claim ownership standing in a *character* apart from a specific published story about the character, so to lay a claim to keeping its lucrative franchise, the company commissioned a series of books using the Hopalong Cassidy character as the hero of the stories. These books, of course, were copyrighted in the company's name, the original author of the series having long since died. In this way, Doubleday hoped to claim ownership of the character without having to pay anyone else a royalty, since the new books were commissioned as works for hire and were written by a young writer whose name appeared nowhere on the books, for the original author's name was still used. The writer, though talented, could not use his own name on a western in any case since it was entirely inappropriate. He used Tex Burns as a name, did his regular books for another publisher and was quite willing to have us put the original author's name on the stories. He seemed to me very good at his craft and I would have liked to have him as a regular, but he didn't want to do any more for us beyond the Hopalong Cassidy books. His real name was Louis L'Amour.

Since that time, it has been well established that a character can stand apart from a specific story and have a legal existence and worth all by itself, as the owners of Mickey Mouse, Sherlock Holmes or Superman will be the first to tell you. This is not the place to go into detail concerning the fine legal points of the matter, but it is an illustration of the fact that an editor of even the most lightly thought of books should have picked up somewhere along the way a working knowledge of the legal atmosphere in which books live. Libel, infringement, the practical meaning of the working of the contract, are matters of great importance, and this is why only the editor in chief usually signs a contract and why any significant departure from the standard wording of a contract occupies the concern of the most senior members of the firm. The little story about Hopalong also explains why every modern contract has wording to the effect that it covers the books in question for all known methods of reproduction "that exist now or may hereafter be invented."

Westerns are also a good example of the truth that no two books are exactly alike, however much they may seem so to an outsider. It would be easy for me to assume that one Harlequin romance is sufficiently like another so that a random selection of any one of them will tell me what they are all like, and in a sense I would be right. The Harlequin editor, though, should be aware that some of them are going to be television movies or series and some are not. He should also be aware that some of the greatest literature has been written within the confines of the closest formulas. A Shakespearian sonnet is written inside one of the most rigid and detailed forms, and yet there is no literature to compare with it. Formulas are therefore not in themselves bad and may, in fact, force a discipline upon an author that is beneficial. The success of a work is not dependent upon its form, but upon the conviction it carries. An editor must learn to sense that conviction whether the author is describing a cattle drive or the retreat from Caporetto. Anyone who cannot feel it—really feel it the way one does music—should not be editing books.

These are digressions. Let us return to thinking about an editor who is handling a department, one perhaps that is presumed not to have much emotion in it—say, the science editor. How does what he is doing differ from what a fiction editor is doing? The answer is, less than you might think, except that he has to keep track of what is going on in a very different field. He will read lots of magazines as well as books published by other firms, and get to know some of the more important figures in the areas in which he is most interested. One person will lead to another and one book will lead to the next one. He must know what he wants and then go out and get it. Does he want to do computer books? He will survey the field and most likely come to the conclusion that not only are there already too many of them but the large majority are not very good, and that there are few if any holes in the market. For him to now go up against people who have a list of computer books and who have had them for years would be foolhardy. So he takes his time and comes to a negative conclusion, prompting his superiors to suspect that he is wasting his time and their money when what he is really doing is his job and saving the firm a lot of grief. Maybe he has spent weeks investigating nothing else and maybe all he has done is take a friend to lunch—wining and dining the editor of computer books for another publisher—but however he has reached his decision, it should be accepted by his colleagues and superiors or else his company should get a new science editor. He should insist and they should accept that he is the only one to make firm decisions in his field for if he can be second-guessed he is useless. Thus, when he has a book he intends to publish, he should have to present it only to the editor-in-chief and the publisher and they should be willing to sign whatever contract he suggests as long as it is within the firm's agreed-to financial parameters.

It is at the level of the senior editor—which is what his title will likely be—that we can begin to think about actual editing. The editor in chief, the executive editor and probably the managing editor are all too busy with corporate matters to actually edit a manuscript. If they have a book that needs to be cut, added to, or rewritten, or to involve them in work on a manuscript page by page, they will not have the time. The manuscript will be handed to someone very junior or else rejected outright, depending on the importance of the author and what is at hand. It is by handling these tasks that young editors gain experience that will stand them well when it comes time to assume more responsibility. Young editors are poorly paid partly because they are not much help until they have been around a while and have done a few of the long, boring jobs they are asked to—and partly because there are so many people willing to do their job for their minimal salary. The senior editor, however, will decide whether he himself will edit a book or give it to a subordinate. A complete rewrite is almost never done inside the house but usually contracted for with a free-lance editor or regular ghost writer. Many of the celebrity biographies that are currently the rage are actually written by a ghost writer, although nowadays, depending on the ego of the celebrity, they may be billed as editor, collaborator, "with the help of" or some other circumlocution. The exact wording of the billing is a weighty matter that will be argued over by the agent for the subject, the agent for the writer, the senior editor, perhaps also the publisher and sales manager and anyone else involved. Suffice it for now to note that these matters are best handled by someone accustomed to diplomacy and someone who enjoys the confidence of the participants—a senior editor at least. The science editor will be no less in need of tact when he has a Nobel Prize winner who is willing to have his name on a book but needs help constructing a readable English sentence.

Below the senior editor there are a number of levels, most of them ill-defined. Some houses observe the distinction of inside editor as against outside editor. The outside man is usually senior—he deals with authors and agents, makes deals, presents the books in sales conference as his, and in general acts as the front man. The inside editor worries about internal matters—the actual preparation of copy, the writing of jacket and promotional material, shepherding the book through the production process, and dealing with an author only insofar as precise details are involved. He nearly always defers to the outside man if there is a decision to make of any substance. Sometimes this editor is called a line editor and sometimes a production editor. A production editor is expected to actually know something about the physical aspects of book production—to know, in fact, as much as any production assistant, and these people usually are needed when a complicated production job is at hand, something like a picture book, a text book, or anything that is not straight text. In a textbook company or an art-book publishing house, almost everybody needs to know production. In a house that does almost nothing but novels, an editor's knowledge of production can be and usually is rudimentary.

It is at this level of editing—which also includes junior editors, associate editors, assistant editors, and sometimes others—that we shall look most closely. It is here that people enter an editorial department, become used to their jobs, learn not only what they need to for their own jobs but also about publishing as a whole process. For the moment, though, we shall leave them to consider one very special member of the fraternity—the copy editor.

Here, for once, is a specific and well-defined job. A copy editor is the person who takes a finished manuscript and checks it for accuracy—punctuation, spelling, correct grammar and internal consistency—and determines whether the author is to be trusted or not. He also marks the manuscript for the typesetter. Although a designer casts off the manuscript and marks it for typeface, lettering size, indentation, spacing, leading (line spacing), folios (page numbers) and display type and the like, the copy editor marks it for capitalization, italics and general style. A book title, for example, can be handled any number of ways. It can be merely capitalized as in A Farewell to Arms, or all caps as in A FAREWELL TO ARMS, or it can be underlined, A Farewell to Arms, or italicized, set in boldface or any number of other styles. The copy editor is concerned that in any given book all book titles be handled the same way. He sees to it that if, say, British spellings are used—cheque for check, honour for honor, zed for zee—then they are consistent throughout. He should have an instinct for misplaced modifiers, dangling participles and split infinitives as well as merely clumsy phrasing or ambiguous statements. Anything that he questions he marks and attaches a query slip to the manuscript page itself to flag for the author. Only after he has had all his queries answered to his satisfaction will the manuscript be released to a designer and typesetter.

The copy editor lives for the triumph of a negative—to be *not* noticed—and this model of self-abnegation must find his satisfaction in correctness, neatness, precision and clarity itself. No one but a good editor and a competent author knows just how valuable he is, and it behooves them both to offer their praise when he has earned it, for praise is the only reward the copy editor can rightly expect. Anyone who wants to know more about what the copy editor does should consult his bible—*The Chicago Manual of Style*, published by the University of Chicago Press. There are other stylebooks, such as *Words Into Type*, but this one seems to be the most widely used.

There is only one area in which the copy editor must, of necessity in a book publishing house, defer to the author, and this is in the question of factual accuracy. In any non-fiction book, history, biography, or any textbook, it is presumed by the reader that the facts have been checked and are accurate, and that the book therefore is to be relied on. In most publishing houses, however, a copy editor simply cannot check everything. Let us say he is editing a civil war history. For him to check every name, every date, every location, in fact, all the assertions made in the text, would be to do the work of author—presumably an authority—all over again, only without his background. He simply cannot check everything, so he is forced to do something else. Most copy editors adopt the tactic of trying to find out how much to trust an author, taking, for instance, the first few pages and checking everything he can. If the author proves to be correct, so far so good. Then the copy editor takes pages at random throughout the book and again checks everything he can. If once more the author proves accurate, the editor has to start to trust him and will then continue going through the book, checking only when something sounds questionable or is seemingly wrong and can be easily checked. It is a matter of his judgment and experience.

Take this passage: "It was raining hard as the morning light roused Jeb Stuart's camp. He scratched his stubble and gave the order for his men to mount at once, for he knew full well how far they must ride before . . ."

Here are any number of facts, some of which can and should be checked and some of which are questionable. 1. Was it raining on the morning of Stuart's famous fatal battle at Yellow Tavern? 2. Were his men in camp in fact and not bivouacked? 3. Did his troop leave at morning light? 4. How far was his camp from the tavern? 5. Did he—could he—have stubble on his chin?

Let us look at each question as a copy editor might. 1. Whether it was in fact raining or not, although it theoretically can be checked, it will not be. Either the editor trusts the author or else it doesn't matter, or it's simply too difficult to check. If the narrative later depends upon the state of the weather and it does matter, perhaps it could be checked. Maybe the horses kept slipping in the mud and progress was retarded. If so, is this the author's fancy or are there other good accounts of the event? 2. The author's story should have made clear the nature of the stay. As long as he is consistent, it won't be checked. 3. When the troop left, and 4. how far they had to go also depend on how much the editor trusts the author. 5. Stubble? This implies a lost shave or two. Here is something that can make an author and his editor look very foolish if they get it wrong. As it happens, it is well known that Stuart was always full bearded. If the copy editor knows this, he will raise a red flag here, and the author will change the phrase to "pulled on his beard." But if Stuart *was* a bearded man, the copy editor should have his confidence in the author shaken indeed, and must be doubly careful. He can easily see the opportunity for sarcasm in a review. "Since Mr. Jones does not seem to know that Stuart was famous for his full beard, it is hardly surprising that his account of the engagement at Yellow Tavern is flawed in other, more serious ways, and . . ." Any competent copy editor, by the way, will have known offhand that Jeb Stuart was actually J.E.B. Stuart and that Jeb is a kind of official nickname and made sure that the author has noted this for the reader long before the account of his last battle. Theoretically, Jeb should be set as "Jeb"—or J.E.B. (Jeb), but no sensible copy editor or author would do either, any more than a sports writer is going to say, "Yesterday, Lawrence P. (Yogi) Berra was named manager of . . ." unless, of course, it's for its presumed humorous effect. Even then, it's questionable.

Here is an example of the copy editor's nightmare:

Steven Runciman, writing in *The American Scholar* about *The Fortification and Defense of Constantinople* by Byron C. P. Tsangadas, says, among other things:

These melancholy reflections are inspired by Mr. Tsangada's work about the walls of Constantinople. Here is a scholar who really knows his subject and has important comments to make on it, but whose book, *The Fortifications and Defense of Constantinople*, is rendered almost valueless by its appalling presentation. The book is rather faintly printed on unattractive paper. We all sadly know that misprints are inevitable nowadays. Even after scrupulous proofreading some still manage to creep in, but there are so many here that one wonders if anyone attempted to proofread the book at all. Even the author's first name is misspelled on the title page. The index is perfunctory and inadequate, and the most deplorable feature is the quality of the maps. A book on the walls of Constantinople which deals with the identification of gates and towers ought to have a really good map of the city. Here we are provided with a map that has been taken from Pere Janin's *Geographie Ecclesiastique de l'Empire Byzantin*. It is an excellent map if reproduced on the scale of the original and if the reader does not mind that names are given in the French form. But it has been reduced to such small dimensions that even with the aid of a magnifying glass most names are completely illegible. There is a sketch of an approximate section and restoration of the walls of Theodosius II, which is copied from Van Millingen's *Byzantine Constantinople: The Walls of the City* and is almost equally illegibly reproduced. There are two plans of sections of the land walls and a rough sketch plan of the Bosporus-

Propontis area. The author in his notes refers at times to maps in other works, notably Schneider's, but they are of little use to the reader who does not have the books at hand.

The author does not help his cause by his writing. His grammar is shaky, and there are some sentences that even lack a verb. It is sometimes impossible to extract any definite meaning from his text. I suppose that it is pedantic to dislike split infinitives, but solecisms such as "neither" followed by "or" recur. There are also frequent repetitions in the text. The author seems to hold with Lewis Carroll's dictum: "What I tell you three times is true." The book appears to have been written in sections, but though Mr. Tsangadas tells us that his research was completed in 1964, he seems never to have taken the time to correlate the various chapters. Had he done so with a critical eye the book would have been much shorter and much more effective. Also, he could then have checked that his use of place-names was consistent. The Blachernae quarter often appears in the text as "Blacherna" and even twice as "Blanchernae."

The most serious decision a copy editor and his senior editor have to make is what to do about an unreliable author. If the copy editor has done enough work on a book to have lost confidence in the author, he then should notify the editor. The two must then decide how important the book is, how important the author is, and how serious the problem is. A lot of very famous authors are really quite sloppy, and both editor and copy editor simply have to live with it and keep as many obvious errors as possible from slipping through to final copy. This is in many ways the worst case. It is actually easier if an author is so sloppy that his work is seen to be hopeless, that is, not fixable by even a good copy editor and not fixable by the author himself. Then a good editor and publisher

104

simply must refuse to proceed with the book as it stands. Perhaps an outside editor can rewrite the book and get it right. If it is an important project, then some corrective deal must be set up. The marginal cases are the hardest to handle—the author says he can fix everything and stands ready to do so, but no one believes he can and will. At that point, the character of the editor is put to the test.

Some years ago, I was the editor of a series of books that came out irregularly but which over the years had added up to a considerable body of work. The books were all in the same format and shared all their important characteristics and all carried similar and easily identifiable titles. One day, an agent called to ask if I would like to commission an addition to the series. He had an author with an established name, although admittedly the name had been established through the publication of different sorts of books. The author wanted to do this job but since he was an established name he would only take it on as a commissioned work. Well, I had always wanted to do this particular book in the series but had never found the right author and I thought, well, maybe. So we all had lunch. He seemed quite convincing, professional and potentially easy to work with. The amount of money the agent was talking about was reasonable. I did want this book, although I had secret doubts about his ability to write it at the level of the rest of the series. I didn't know, though, of anyone else who could do it, and certainly didn't know of anyone who could be trusted to do it better. I signed it up.

About a year later, the manuscript of the great book appeared. I read it carefully, and was profoundly disappointed. The work was shallow in the extreme, was written with no style or verve, and failed to convey conviction or enthusiasm for the subject. I had doubts as to its reliability—although there was no specific thing that I could spot that was incorrect or inaccurate. All in all, I realized that I had a book on my desk that I would have turned down if it had just come through the door unsolicited. I would have advised the author to go back and study the project and everything about it for another fifteen or twenty years and then perhaps the requisite sense of erudition and deep familiarity with the subject would begin to show. As it was, I didn't know what to do.

On the side against publishing, there were a number of considerations. The first and most important was that this book was simply not up to the standard that had been established by the series, and by publishing it I would be demeaning all the rest of the books, whether anyone else knew that or not. I had no particular love for or continuing relationship with the author. He wasn't going to write other books for me as he already had a regular publisher for the books by which he had made his name. A publishing house will make a lot of allowances for a favorite or reliably money-making author, but this one was neither. The *need* to publish this book didn't exist. I could afford to wait until a more appropriate author came along. Although if I turned down this manuscript, we would have laid out a certain amount of money, it wasn't a huge sum. The book, if we did not do it, would probably not find another publisher, so we wouldn't get our money back. Even so, it wasn't any amount that should sway our basic decision. I feared a snide and nasty review that pointed out a lot of errors and omissions and made clear that my author hadn't read all the other work in this field. That would damage the reputation of the series as a whole and could prove truly costly, and I simply couldn't feel confident that I was not running that risk. I knew that, in fact, if I published, I *would* be running that risk.

On the side of going ahead with it was that I had commissioned the work, that the author had an established name, that few if any reviewers would know enough about the subject to spot errors and omissions, and that there would be the very devil to pay if I decided against it. My publisher would want to know why in hell I deliberately threw money away by first going after the book and then changing my mind. If I didn't like it all that much, so what? Couldn't it be published and ride along on the reputation of the series as a whole? Where would we get our money back if we turned it down? When would that agent ever offer us another book if we said no? Wasn't I being artsy-fartsy as an editor? Wouldn't it sell and make money regardless of what I thought about it?

I wrestled with myself and made the kind of decision any man of character would—I equivocated. I gave it to the best copy editor I knew and warned him that I was suspicious of it, and that he should check it as closely as he knew how. If it was full of holes, I would have to think about turning it down outright, but if it stood up to really careful scrutiny, then I might go ahead. In the end he gave it, surprisingly, a clean bill of health, and I swallowed hard and went ahead. It was published in due course and we got away with it. It sold, it never drew a bad notice, and the only person who wasn't happy was me. Such are the rewards of character.

It should be noted that, in what has gone before, we are talking about trade books. The situation is much more serious in textbooks and scholarly publishing, and there a copy editor's responsibility is magnified considerably, so much so that the regular editor will often do for his books much of what a copy editor would in a trade house. Similarly, on a magazine, if the magazine has pretensions of seriousness, there is usually a department devoted to getting the facts right. *The New Yorker* checking department, for example, is famous, and rightly so.

Here is the kind of thing that keeps coming up. In an article in *Sail* magazine for December 1985, entitled "Barebones Cruising" by David Buckman, we find this sentence: "While those who insist upon a contemporary definition of comfort might find a rather spartan flavor to existence aboard the barebones cruiser, as Thoreau observed, 'Most of the luxuries, and many of the so-called comforts of life, are not only indispensable, but positive hinderances to the elevation of mankind.' "

Did Thoreau say "indispensable" or did he say "dispensable"? They have opposite meanings and the correct meaning from the context would be "dispensable." Do you know Thoreau well enough to know where to find that quote? It sounds like it is from *Walden,* but without reading the complete works of Thoreau of which *Walden* is only a small part, are you even willing to read through *Walden* again to get this right? Should you query the author? Well, you would have gotten an A on this quiz if you had 1. Noticed the questionable word to begin with, 2. Decided not to reread *Walden,* and 3. Queried the author and refused to let the word go through until you got an answer.

And remember, in this quiz you weren't even asked the following questions, because any good copy editor would know the answer offhand. Should "spartan" be capitalized? Should the word "Most"—which starts the quote— be capitalized? Does it start a sentence in the original, and if so, should it be kept capitalized if it is used, as it is here, in a longer sentence? Is the quote correctly punctuated? Should the punctuation of the original, however bizarre, be followed if that is what the original was? Should "barebones" really be used as one word? Isn't that an affectation? Isn't "bare bones" correct? Should the word "definition" be questioned? Wouldn't "level" perhaps be better? If all these questions as well as their answers had naturally come to you as you read the quote, then you should think of applying for a copy editor's job. Just for interest, the actual quote is as follows:

"Most of the luxuries, and many of the so called comforts of life, are not only not indispensable, but positive hinderances to the elevation of mankind."*

Note that the magazine version has inserted a hyphen between "so" and "called," which doesn't change the meaning much but is still not correct. It has also dropped a crucial "not," thus changing both the tone and meaning of the whole sentence. The capitalization and punctuation are correctly followed.

Such, then, are the easily defined positions in the editorial department. We will now try and look at what might be called the junior editor.

In any consideration of the ordinary working editor, it must be said at the outset that, before anything else, they vary a lot. No general discussion is likely to enable you to recognize the particular editor with whom you find yourself working. Even though their tastes, temperaments, backgrounds and knowledge can be startling in their range, nonetheless, they will share some common characteristics that can be understood by outsiders or emulated by those hoping to get a similar job.

In the first place, young editors can be expected to be pretty bright and pretty well read. People who run edi-

*From *The Annotated Walden*, by Henry David Thoreau, edited, with an introduction, notes and bibliography, by Philip Van Doren Stern (Clarkson N. Potter, Inc., New York, 1970), page 155.

torial departments will almost never hire someone who isn't at least seen to have a minimum background. How smart and how well read they are will come out in their reader's reports over a few months. In any editorial department, people who are being considered for permanent jobs in the department will usually be given a trial period when they read manuscripts that are submitted, proposals that have come in from agents, or books that are actually in the publishing process.

Here it is necessary to pause and consider the central internal document of the publishing house—the reader's report. The most important document bearing on the external life of a house is, of course, the contract. The reader's report is the most important document bearing on the internal workings of the house. Any editor, no matter what his position and no matter what the book may be, will usually write a reader's report on any book that is being considered by the firm. The typical report will explain briefly what the book is, and what the editor thinks of it. The report should also include whatever publishing considerations are relevant, since this report and others written by different editors will be used to form the decision about it that will be taken at the editorial meeting. The publishing considerations will include the author's history, his possible future, the expected level of advance and royalties wanted, and anything else helpful or harmful. Helpful considerations would include magazine serials, book club interest, promotion possibilities and prospects, or anything else that will help sales. Harmful considerations might include other books in direct competition with this one, an author who cannot or will not help with promotion, or perhaps subject matter that largely precludes book club and reprint possibilities. The editor who could be expected to handle the book if it is taken would be the one to write the most detailed report—the one which includes the publishing factors. Other reports would be more brief and only include the editor's opinion of the project.

Within an editorial department, the basic reader's report will be attached to the manuscript and go to the next editor. He will add his report, and so it will go until enough reports have been attached to make a decision possible. Obviously a new book by an established author who is regularly handled by a senior person will have only one report—by the editor who handles that author. Only if a new or very different financial deal is asked for will there be any need for other opinions. Say an author's agent suddenly asks for dramatically improved terms. Can the new book justify them? Does the editor involved want to take sole responsibility for a big new raise in the stakes of the game? He probably doesn't, so before anyone decides anything, other opinions are solicited.

Every publishing house has its own special routine, and in many of them the most senior people don't bother to write reports. It is safe to say, though, that a new book turning up in an editorial department that is read by a junior editor who thinks it has some possibility of being published will in fact have a report written about it. In some houses, a book that is obviously going to be rejected will simply be rejected—even though the editor may write a letter to the author or agent about it. In other houses, all books that come in must have some sort of report made on them before they go out. This practice has put a crimp in the career of more than one young editor, for nothing is more embarrassing than having written a two-line dismissal of a book and sent it back only to have the book turn up on the best-seller list a year later. A book that has been widely turned down and afterward becomes notable is a special delight for anyone who hates editors—and it seems that there are a lot who do. Books like that always get a lot of publicity. What does not get so much notice is that for every book a young editor was wrong about, there will most likely be several dozen he was right about.

In any case, a young editor who is writing several brief reports a day or a lengthy and thoughtful report every few days is also writing reports on himself, whether he knows it or not. Books are often understood in comparison with or in contrast to other books. Reports will often have phrases like "This reads very much like the young . . ." or "The style will seem familiar to anyone who knows . . ." or "This is better than . . . (citing a recent best-seller)", or "This author has the potential of becoming the equal of . . .". If within a couple of weeks an editor's reports contain dazzling references to a wide range of modern literature, easy familiarity with current pop culture, and a mature understanding of classical writing, others will soon notice. If the reports are badly written, shallow in their judgment, and offer no comparisons except to, say, the world of sports, then it is very likely that the young person will quickly find a job in one of the business departments.

Traditionally, the route up for women has been through a secretarial job to an editor, and for a man a job in sales. For the woman, the transition up is natural and easy as she gradually takes on more and more responsibility from her boss, who learns to trust her ability by seeing it at work from day to day. Women thus tend to train women, but men may find themselves training their secretaries as well. It is perhaps for this reason that thirty years ago the ratio of male to female in a big editorial department was about fifty-fifty, whereas now it is likely to be two or three to one female. Then and now it was understood that most books are bought by women, but now it seems there is more willingness to let women edit them also.

Today, people with aspirations to becoming a book editor seem to have become impatient and want to get jobs as editors more or less straight out of college. This is ill-advised, both from their own point of view and from that of the publishing house. Most editors make a career of being an editor, so that once they make it to that level, they usually stay there. This means that what rough and tumble in business they ever learn will have to be learned before they start being an editor. For this reason, very few, if any, men start out as editors. Their paths up will most often begin somewhere in sales. In textbook companies, they will have been on the road for a considerable length of time. In trade book companies, they may have been on the road or worked in bookstores or perhaps in advertising and promotion. Whatever job they have held, they will have made use of the opportunity to recommend books, to comment on books that the firm publishes, to meet authors, and to become familiar with the whole publishing process. If they just wish to be salesmen—and many salesmen are perfectly happy to make that a career—then all they need to do is their regular job.

It should be noted in passing that salesmen, especially good ones, are a self-selected lot. They usually make good money, like the life, and not only have little interest in but also actively avoid the petty squabbles and politics that pervade the home office. They tend to see themselves as much more free and independent than office workers, and it is by no means unusual for a salesman to refuse a promotion to sales manager. A young editor is well advised to get to know the salesmen who sell the firm's books. Their advice carries significant weight, and their experience can be called upon from time to time by an editor who still lacks his own. It is, in fact, quite important for a young editor to establish himself in a position of friendship and trust with his salesmen, for if he does not, his books could well be slighted in favor of those being handled by more congenial editors. Professional respect can only be built up over a period of years, so it is well to start with friendship. Salesmen don't really have much more of an idea of what an editor does all day than an ordinary businessman does, but they do know that their popularity in the field depends heavily on how good the books are that they sell. An editor who produces winners will find himself offered plenty of drinks at the bar at sales conferences, but one who keeps overselling dull books will earn only polite nods.

For a man, then, experience in business or in selling is almost a prerequisite for an editorial job. There is no more telling way to open an editorial discussion than by saying, "Well, when I was managing a bookstore, we found that . . ." or "When I was on the road, most of the big buyers always said that . . ." The one thing that everybody is supposed to be looking for is sales. Many editors are not in fact expecting much in the way of sales for some books, but that is never a point that they will or should admit. All must appear to be attuned to maximum sales, so an argument made from a sales perspective is usually a very strong one. Anyone with direct experience in sales always has an edge over someone who has never strayed from the editorial desk.

If one were to give advice as to what kind of education a young person ought to get if his ultimate aspiration was to become a book editor, it would have to be that of a broad liberal education. Today, a masters degree or even a doctorate gives one a leg up, especially in textbook houses, but

114

even in that case, one's education should not be too narrow. A specialist in Restoration comedy is not of much help in a publishing house, whereas someone who has studied philosophy or history can be very useful. Even though it is likely that any given editor will eventually drift into somewhat specialized kinds of books, in the beginning of a career all sorts of varied tasks will present themselves, and a young editor should not shirk any of them.

One young editor with whom I worked some years ago was given the thankless task of getting a politician's speeches in shape for book publication. A flinty millionaire was promoting a certain public figure for a presidential campaign, so a book of the great man's sayings naturally was required. The publishing house, guaranteed of a very large order for the book from the millionaire, was only too happy to publish, especially because the president of the company himself thought the candidate should be elected. Commerce and public spirit thus both being satisfied, the young editor was handed a batch of speeches and asked to pull together a book. It happened that the candidate was an unusually boring, vapid and empty-headed fellow, so doing anything with his speeches was a truly numbing job, but the young editor did it as asked and soon discovered that in doing so he had established a direct line of communication with the president of the company. Other young editors would never dream of picking up the office phone and calling the president—it took quite a bit of nerve to ask anything of their direct superior—so the young man who knew the president found himself suddenly quite well placed to promote his projects. If he walked into a superior's office and said, "Oh, by the way, the president has asked me to look into this proposal for him, and I wonder if I could ask you to

. . ." then he would get what he wanted. Imagine the difference if he could only say, "Look, I have this idea, and I wonder if you'd like to read it over and . . ." In that case the senior would most likely say, well, okay, I'll have a look at it in due course, but don't hold your breath for an answer. He wouldn't mention that he would also consider it in the light of what it might do to his own position and career, and not necessarily only on its merits. Such are office politics, and such are the variety of lessons available to young people.

Let us, then, consider a young man who has the job of associate editor in the editorial department of the Mill & Mine Publishing Company, Inc., a fully diversified enterprise comprising textbooks, both college and graduate level, children's books and trade books. He is to be the assistant to the executive editor of the Trade Department. He has served his apprenticeship by first working in and then handling a department of the bookstore at the college where he studied. It was a respectable but by no means famous college, where he majored in European history and specialized in the intellectual history of Europe from 1815 to 1914. After college he briefly took a job with Bed & Breakfast, Inc., which sold guidebooks to inexpensive places to stay on the East Coast, but seeing no future in that, he soon took a job with an outfit of independent sales representatives who handled the lines of a number of small publishers. He had the southern territory, based in Atlanta, and did that for three years until Mill & Mine offered him a job on their sales staff. At Mill & Mine, he took the trouble to write memos to editors when he found out something useful about a book. He passed along to the department a couple of pretty good manuscripts, one that had come from a bookstore manager whom he knew and another from one of his old professors at college. One was

116

published and did fairly well, well enough so that the author's next book might have a chance to break into the big time. The young man was offered an editorial job after only two and a half years selling in the Midwest for Mill & Mine. Now what will happen?

As a young editor, he soon discovers that his opinion is in demand from all the other young editors. Having been in sales, whatever he says about a book that sounds positive will carry some weight, so his more senior colleagues soon put on his desk all their favorite projects, which he has to read and write reports on. His immediate boss, the executive editor, handles some of the biggest names that the house publishes, and they take up a lot of his time, so he often asks his assistant to take care of the details when it comes to his less important people. The young man, in effect, becomes the editor for his superior's newer and younger authors. Doing this means writing internal reports and copy for other departments, sales pitches, catalog copy, perhaps preliminary jacket copy, and he finds himself in charge of production estimates and scheduling for his own books as well as the executive editor's.

One of the first things that strikes him—he is very bright and ambitious, after all—is that most of the people in his department have little or no say in how their books get designed and how they are priced. He knows from having watched the process hundreds of times, that people who are handed a book usually heft it in their hand, flip through it to get a general idea of how it looks, and check the price before they even read anything but the title. He knows that a lousy-looking book that carries a high price doesn't sell as well as a good-looking book that seems to offer reasonable value for money. He is thus surprised at how indifferent most editors, especially fiction editors, seem to be about such matters. He finds that the art department does the design and the sales department sets the price. The production department tells the sales department what the book will cost, based on the art department specifications and the size of the first printing. In all of this, the editorial department seems to have little say. Why is that?

The fact is that not many editors view their work as the exercise of a craft, and their knowledge and understanding of what goes on in other departments is often superficial at best. The young editor sees this and silently deplores it and asks if he can enroll in a couple of night courses. His department head is delighted and offers to pay the tuition, so he takes a course in book design and another in book production. These prove to be very useful because he soon is able to talk to the designer of his books in a way they both understand, and to the production department people in terms that they understand. Before long, in an entirely informal way, he is having a significant if not decisive word in how his own books are manufactured and priced. Since he came from sales, no one thinks twice if he comments on pricing, so he feels free to do that in meetings, but the other matters are left out of open discussion and depend more on knowing the people in the other departments and getting along with them.

Little by little, then, the young editor gets established in his position and gains working relationships with those around him and in other departments. But how, having become effective inside the house, can he now start to establish his standing outside the house? He certainly does not want to be just an assistant to a big-time editor. He intends to be holding a position such as that himself in another dozen years, aiming, say, to be a senior editor with a major title by the time he is forty. He sees that the only way that this is possible is for him to have his own list of books and authors—people he has brought in and handled and made successful. It is all very well to be a protégé of a senior man, and to learn all that you can from him, but he is still in his twenties and his boss is well into his fifties. Only when the young editor can stand on his own, without any protection, will he be able to command the respect, the influence and the salary that should be his due by then.

This is perhaps not the place to examine the theory and practice of the mentor-student relationship, except to note that it is very common in large organizations, and rightly so, or else each new generation would never get proper training. It is, however, a delicate relationship for the student, more delicate perhaps than the parent-child relationship, as it is open and voluntary rather than being natural and to some degree out of awareness. It thus behooves the student to tread a fine line between undue deference and overobvious self-reliance. Tact, restraint and sophistication are the keys—and those who have these will make the transitions easily, while those who do not may find the path upward blocked or be inexplicably turned aside. Do not spurn the teacher, but do not become his slave.

At this point, we are at the heart of why too many books get published in this country and why too many of them aren't very good. The younger editor must build his own list, and the only way he can do it is with new authors and new books. Partly out of youthful enthusiasm, he will think more of a book than a jaded reviewer will, but more out of the need to find and nurture talent will he take a chance where an older hand will pass.

Leaving our special young man and thinking of all those in his position, we can think about how young editors all work to establish themselves even as they do their jobs.

They meet authors and learn how to handle them, finding that authors have a much wider range of variation than do young editors, and that if tact is required inside the house, a double dose is needed outside. They meet the agents who represent the authors they get to know, and by doing so build a working relationship for the future. They go to the meetings of publishing groups and meet people who are working in other houses. This is more important than anyone ever explains to them. Some editors are going to become the proverbial much-traveled editor whose career takes him first to one house and then to another, so those transitions will be much eased by knowing people around town. But it is really not so much for future jobs that knowing people is useful as it is for the exchange of ideas and books. A not inconsiderable number of books are sent to one publishing house and rejected, but rejected with the comment that although this particular house is not a candidate for this book, perhaps sending it down the street to so-and-so at Mill & Mine might be a good idea. If half a dozen young editors around town know that our special young man is a specialist in the intellectual history of nineteenth-century Europe, then they will now and then steer something his way that may be of special import to him. Only a few such contacts need work because, ideally at least, one book leads to an author who will do more books and that author may also lead to other authors.

Here it is perhaps well to repeat some advice that was given me by my boss and mentor when I was young. If I intended to get ahead, I should remember two things. The first was to never refuse responsibility. If someone asks if you will do a job, always say yes. If you don't know how to do it, find out, but never appear unwilling to shoulder a burden. Second, always make a friend for the house. No contact that you make outside the house should result in anything other than a new friend for it. Ken McCormick was then and now famous because he was so deft at turning people down that even when he said no they felt as good as when he said yes. A friend made has the same effect as dropping a pebble in a pool—the ripples silently spread out and cover the whole surface. Some houses are fortunate in having editors who make friends of whomever they're in contact with, while others fail to realize that some editors can be like cancers eating away at the reservoir of goodwill the house may have built up over many years. These two ideas have served me well, and they should both be firmly implanted in the consciousness of any young editor who intends to make a successful career.

Suppose now that we have our young man in a good junior editorial job and that he is so far doing all the right things. He is taking courses, meeting people, practicing tact, reading huge stacks of stuff, working without thought of anything but what relates to his job, and in all respects being the very model of a potential star. What do they look for? How do they decide what to work on? We already know that each must develop his own list, but how do they do that?

It is at this point that a good agent or a young writer enters. A young writer needs someone who believes not only in his book at hand but also in his future. Look at the first books that were published by people who later became famous. A lot of them were merely promising. Once in a while, a writer like Truman Capote will publish a book that makes him famous overnight, but this is rare, and it is far more usual for fame to come slowly. This means that someone has recognized talent and bet on it, sometimes

121

suffering through disappointing results for a book or two, but doing so in the hope and belief that the author's promise makes the whole thing worthwhile.

When Jim Silberman was a young editor at Dial, he had to handle a book called *Giovanni's Room* by James Baldwin. It presented a problem. Baldwin had published *Go Tell It on the Mountain* three years before, and it had been a smashing success for a first book, putting his name on the map and making excellent money. Silberman believed in Baldwin's future as a writer and wanted to keep him at Dial, but there were two serious hitches. The first was that Dial at the time was in very shaky financial shape and could ill afford the luxury of publishing a book that might not even make back its expenses—and that seemed a real possibility. The second was that the book was a more or less self-indulgent look at homosexuality in Paris. Homosexuality was at the time firmly in the closet and not considered a topic for polite conversation, let alone suitable as the central subject of a novel. The owner of The Dial Press didn't like either Baldwin's admission of his own homosexuality or the book itself, let alone the perceived fruity waft of scent that it would wash across both the name of the publishing house and his own as its owner. Silberman made his plea for publication on the basis of the book being something we had to suffer through in order to keep Baldwin, because if we refused it, someone else would certainly take it on the same grounds and Baldwin would be gone. Dial didn't have that many people to count on as future stars, so it could not afford to miss what could be a big one. All in all, a hard choice, but we did publish the book, and it did get very lukewarm reviews as well as some really bad ones, and we just sold enough, as I recall, to about break even. In this case, Silberman was right, because Baldwin did go on to become rich and famous, and he did stay with Dial, even though the company itself was sold in the meantime and Silberman left as well.

The foregoing is an illustration of a number of points. If Baldwin's name had not been on that manuscript and it had come in from an unknown, it would undoubtedly have been rejected. It stands as a good example of why some not very good books do get published. There is also no guarantee of loyalty or gratitude. All a publisher can do is *hope* that an author will stay with him. As we have already seen, no option clause is really binding, so this is also an example of a gamble on what are usually long odds. Further, it is an example of a subject that is distasteful to many involved with it, which is aired for reasons that have nothing to do with the subject itself. If politics makes strange bedfellows, so does hope.

But now let us consider how a young editor goes about moving the people around him to do what he has decided he wants. Say that he has found a book that others have spurned.

There is a good recent case study of this in *Adrift* by Steven Callahan, a story of survival at sea by a young man who was adrift for seventy-six days before being rescued. In a large feature article about the book that appeared in *The Providence Journal* of January 16, 1986, we read that "Publishers did not pursue him. Several turned him down. Last year, he brought his book to Houghton Mifflin Company in Boston which, after editing and instructing him to write a new first chapter and an epilogue, is giving it the big push, sending it out to reviewers with full brochure and sending Callahan on a ten-city tour to promote it." This reveals a lot. It means that an editor looked at a flawed manuscript that others had not noticed, perhaps not having gotten past the first chapter—note that his publisher asked for a new *first* chapter—and saw possi-bilities. He must have written an enthusiastic report and made specific recommendations and gotten others to read it and share his belief that there was something valuable here.

In any house, it is this process of persuading many people to read a book and begin to share a feeling of enthusiasm and possibility that is the crucial step by step building of an edifice of belief that turns into action. The decision to do a full brochure and to do an author trip did not happen without a further buildup within the house after the editors had taken the book, gotten it revised as they thought would help it most, and then persuaded others to read it and think of its possibilities. From the day a first reader looked at a much traveled manuscript by an unknown person who had never written a book before to the day a full-page feature about it appeared in a paper that is dominant in its region, an almost uncountable number of small steps had to have been taken, each one reinforcing those before. Included in these steps were a sale of a piece of the book to *Sail* magazine—a first serial sale which alerts readers of the magazine to a good sea story, and gives them a taste of it well before the book itself appears. Then there is the sale of a book club edition to the Dolphin Book Club, specialists in books about boats and the sea. Just when the decision was made to do a full brochure (a quite rare thing) and to do an author tour would be hard to say from the outside—it may be hard to pinpoint even from the inside—but would have come along when salesmen read the book, early reviews came in, and perhaps when the magazine sale was made.

At some point the work gets taken out of the hands of its original editor and becomes the concern of the house as a whole—and this, after all, is the editor's aim, although it is an aim that is not often realized. Let us say that the book sells well and has a fine paperback sale as well. Everyone will be happy, and the editor will reap his reward in the future, when his opinions are not only given more weight than they used to be given, but also allow him to write in his reports such things as, "Like *Adrift* when we first saw it, this needs to . . ." or "This probably has at least as much potential as *Adrift* when we first saw it . . ." If Steven Callahan decides to do further books, he will find an enthusiastic editor.

In passing, it is worth noting that while *Adrift* can only have a positive effect on the career of whoever was its champion at Houghton Mifflin, its effect on the careers of those that failed to see its possibilities is much more problematic. If an editor at another house saw it and promptly sent it back without showing it to anyone else, possibly it will have no adverse effect, for no one will realize what has been missed. If, however, an editor liked it and showed it around his department, let us hope that he got a number of reports on it before sending it back. Only if several people have agreed upon a decision can it be seen as essentially not the editor's fault that their collective wisdom turned out to be wrong. A young editor must thus know his own mind and show things to his colleagues only if he is pretty well sure that he has something good. It is really very rare for anyone to check back later and see whether a best-seller has been around and rejected. It does happen, though, and it is to avoid that fate that many young editors would rather publish questionable books than miss a best-seller. The central truth is that when you take on a book, you don't know what is going to happen to it. It is only after you are committed to the publishing process that you find out its actual potential.

The number of small decisions that will have been made

in the course of publishing *Adrift* will almost all have been taken at some meeting or other, and the book's editor may well have had meetings about the jacket, about subsidiary rights sales, about an advertising budget, about promotion (the brochure and the author trip). All of those after the editorial meetings that settled on taking the book in the first place. And this is only one book. Obviously, then, a young editor must spend a lot of time in meetings, and this is the norm, much to the annoyance of their authors, agents, wives and friends. No general understanding of what happens in publishing can be arrived at without an understanding of the uses and management of meetings.

Ostensibly and officially, the reason for holding meetings is to have a whole department make decisions at a time when the collective knowledge and experience can be brought to bear on what is decided. Decisions which commit the money, time and talents of a large organization to any given course of action cannot be taken either lightly or without the knowledge of all those thus committed. The central meeting of the publishing house is the editorial meeting at which contracts are discussed and agreed upon. The decision to publish or not to publish and the royalty rates and amount of money committed to the advance and possibly later to the advertising and promotion budget all may be decided upon in the basic editorial committee meeting.

It should be noted in passing that a big advance necessarily involves the house in a big publishing effort, whereas a small advance can be earned back with a much more routine publishing job—a point not lost on agents. Also, deciding to do an art book that will sell for $50 is committing much more money to production than deciding to do a $15 novel, a point that is surprisingly often forgotten by all concerned.

The people in the editorial meeting will, of course, be the editors, or at least the senior editors. Publishing houses seem to run in cycles—from holding meetings to which almost everybody is invited to those to which a severely limited group may attend. Typically, though, all senior editors and anyone who can negotiate a contract will be invited. Assistants and juniors may be allowed to attend but not to speak in the hope that what they hear will prove educational. Usually the sales manager, the financial manager, or moneyman (whether he is called publisher, group chief, president, or whatever) and the advertising and subsidiary rights people will all attend. The meeting is or should be run by the editor in chief, but, if not, then by the moneyman. He will solicit each speaking member in turn and see what he or she has to propose. Others will comment on the proposals, and a decision may be arrived at or deferred for further work or opinions. In theory, anyone who has helpful knowledge or a previously unannounced opinion will voice it and add to the range of collective wisdom until a sense of the meeting is clear enough, the decision is recorded, and the next matter of business comes up. The level of formality varies greatly from place to place and even from time to time, but it is from these meetings that the course of action of the whole publishing company will proceed.

Young editors with any insight will soon realize that the ostensible reasons for holding a meeting have almost nothing to do with the real ones. The actual reason for holding a big formal meeting is to spread responsibility around to enough people so that if a decision should prove to be wrong there will have been so many people involved with it that no one of them can be singled out for blame. Further, meetings are not for making decisions but for ratifying them. The only real function of a meeting is its use as a method of education and to insure that internal information is conveyed to those who need it. In large organizations, there is often no way for the left hand to know what the right hand is doing, and poor internal communication very often robs the group of effectiveness. It is a constant and regular hazard in any and every enterprise, and meetings are one of the most effective ways to get everybody to know what decision has been taken and understand what consequences that will have for whatever part of it each member has to carry out. A decision once taken in a large open meeting is later very hard to change, and the consequences that will flow from it will be around for a long time, especially in book publishing, so it behooves all those concerned to make the best possible decisions. That is why real decision making is too important to be left to the vagaries of an open meeting.

The basic rule is that unless specifically requested to do so by a superior, you should never attend a meeting that has an uncertain outcome. If you are not absolutely sure in your own mind exactly what will happen in that meeting—as it pertains to you, of course—then figure out a way to stay away from the question and organize it better for next time. If you are planning to present *Adrift*, you will have at hand not only your own detailed report, which has already been seen by a number of your colleagues, but also several of their supporting reports. You will know that your immediate boss is all for the proposal. You will have talked to the author or his agent and found out how big an advance is needed, what royalty terms are in negotiation, and whether the author is willing and able to do what you think is needed (a new opening chapter and an epilogue). In short, by the time you speak in an open meeting, for all practical purposes the decisions have already been made. The only real reason for attending the meeting is to make everything official and to let everybody know you think you have a hot one going. Sales, advertising and rights managers now hear about your find, and when the rights person lands the *Sail* magazine article, there will be another meeting to discuss how to build on that. That you can't know about until it happens—although some books have already been sold to a magazine when the publisher takes them—and in this case you are taking a book that is not yet in shape to show outside.

The central point is that it is distressing if not damaging to an editor to go into a meeting, make a proposal, and have it rejected. If that happens often, others might come to the conclusion that perhaps that editor ought to be doing a different job, something like installing telephones. It is of the utmost importance to a young career not to have to suffer rejection in public, and so the acquisition and practice of what are essentially political skills are necessary. It is also well to remember that if no one likes being shot down in public, no one likes the shooter either. Lifelong enmities have been established that way.

There are some simple things that everyone may do to ease the pain of meetings and conform to the rituals they present. The first of these is to ask for more than you expect to get. If you know you can get a book for ten thousand in advance, and that is a firm figure, then just say so. If you haven't finished negotiating and don't really know at what point the thing may end, ask for enough. It is very poor technique to say that you think that you can sign it up for ten thousand and then not be able to. If you say that you think you may have to go to fifteen and get authorization to do so, then when you come in and report

129

you got it for twelve-five, everyone will be pleased. If you say you think you can get it for ten but may have to go to twelve-five, and then indeed do have to go to twelve-five, few will be at all impressed. If you say you think it's worth ten and that the firm shouldn't offer more, and then when the agent says he won't take less than twelve-five, you appear to be incompetent. The direct costs of publishing are going to be some forty or fifty thousand dollars and here you are about to lose a book over two and a half thousand dollars. You have to go back to the meeting and get the ceiling raised to twelve-five, and no one will thank you. And all this range of impressions as to your competence are based on a book that has the same advance—namely twelve-five.

Next, be very very careful in offering criticism and only a little less careful in offering praise. If your praise has the effect of taking someone's book away from him, he won't thank you. If you reinforce the approval you have already voiced in your written report, that's fine—but never change your mind. If your position can't be counted on, no one will seek it.

If someone makes a stupid suggestion, one that you know for sure is a disaster, don't shoot it down in public. Find a ruse to do more study on the question and get the decision delayed, and then make your criticism in person and not in writing. Keep it strictly between yourselves, and your colleague undoubtedly will end up thanking you. But don't do it at all unless you are sure.

Finally and always and most important—do your homework. Imagine yourself listening to the presentation that is about to take place and think what questions would occur to you to ask, and think up everything that anybody could possibly ask, and then get the answers ready. It is far better to walk out of a meeting with half the things you know never having come to light than to walk out with a specific assignment to go find out something that you hadn't thought to prepare. If you are consistently seen to have the relevant answers ready whenever a reasonable question is asked, then your career is on a firm road upward, and confidence in your judgment will be building bit by bit. People who never come in with their answers prepared stay junior editors for a long time.

The usual questions that should be answered in a reader's report or which an editor should be prepared to answer in an editorial meeting are:

1. What is the market for this book? Who is going to read it? Who is going to want to pay to have it?
2. Is there a clear path to reaching the market? (In the case of *Adrift*, the answer to both the questions are positive and easy. In the case of a first novel, the answer must necessarily be far harder.)
3. Are there other books to which this one can be compared?
4. What does this book have that others don't?
5. What is the existing competition?
6. What is the author's history, reputation and expected future?
7. What can be said now about promotion, publicity and subsidiary sales?

If a young editor is not ready to answer any of these questions in an open meeting, then he is not ready to present the book at all.

Before leaving the subject of meetings, it is perhaps not inappropriate to consider the matter of running them. The man who runs the meeting has a delicate job and those who do it well are rare. It is an art, and like any art can only be learned by long practice and a deep understanding of what is going on and what needs to be accomplished. People who are good at conducting meetings in such a way that most participants come out of them satisfied and with a feeling of accomplishment are the same people to whom very serious responsibility is entrusted. Running a good meeting is the mark of a seasoned and capable executive, and the youthful aspirer should notice the technique with care. The trick of a good meeting is to keep it on track and yet let everyone have a sense that he or she is adding something to it. Knowing when to turn off a long-winded commentator, when and how to keep the discussion relevant to the issue at hand, how to avoid open conflict but not squelch reasonable criticism, and how to keep matters at a pace that gets things done but doesn't make people feel pressured, these are the things to look for. If a meeting lets someone ramble on at length, avoids and defers decisions, fails to cover a significant part of the agenda, or allows personal feelings to boil up, then everyone will feel frustrated and angry and the meeting may as well not have taken place. To control it but not to turn it into a lockstep march, to hear thoughtfully made comments, and to consider even seemingly outlandish suggestions, but not to frighten or ridicule the young or unseasoned or misinformed, these should be the aim of the professional.

A young person can make quite an accurate judgment of the overall ability of a senior executive by finding out how all the younger people in the department feel about attending one of his meetings. If it an occasion for wit and banter, but nonetheless a test of how sharp one is today, then the signs are good. If it is seen to be a drag and a bore to be suffered through, then the signs are very poor. A young person can in quiet and subtle ways influence who will become his mentor. Everyone wants to hitch his wagon to a star, but there are all kinds of stars, including novas, pulsars, and those that burn hard, steady and long.

The most critical part of an editor's job is the handling of his authors and their agents. It is extremely important that they should come to trust him and to feel that he is their best advocate inside the house. To them he must seem their best friend at court and the only one to whom they would want to turn if they need something from the house. Note that an author, especially if his book is a success, will meet any number of people within the house, from his copy editor to the production people and the publicity people, and the author may well have the choice of asking for things directly from any one of them. If his relationship with his editor is shaky or unsatisfactory, then he may try going directly to any of these people—but if that happens, everybody is in trouble. The internal people will never be sure of how to handle a request, or how much to tell an author, and usually some sort of disaster will take place. An editor should enjoy the confidence of his own people as well as his authors, and thus everything should go through him. He should make the judgment as to when to convey bad news, or whether to convey it at all, when and how to break good news, and whether and how to honor requests.

Take, for example, the sale of a book club edition. If the rights manager thinks a deal is a good possibility, the editor usually will be told. But the editor should never get his author's hopes up unless the final outcome is going to be favorable. It is only when the editor *knows* that he should tell his author that there *may* be a deal. Rights managers who deal with book clubs on a daily basis know that a sale is made when it is agreed upon over the phone, even though the formal letter of agreement may not be in fact signed for a matter of weeks, so when the rights manager makes one, the editor can, and should, be told. Then he can play it any way he wants, remembering that raising false hopes is always destructive, and taking good news too casually is equally hurtful. It ultimately is the editor, not the rights manager, who should decide how to handle the good news. He knows his author best, and should know how to make the most of it. A seasoned professional who always gets a club deal is very different from a panicky and ultranervous first novelist to whom the news of a club deal may be the greatest thing he has ever heard. For him, the club deal may, in fact, mark the turning point in a whole career, and his editor ought to understand that and deal with it accordingly—lunch at a good restaurant and a nice bottle of wine would not be out of place. The editor, after all, will be celebrating as much for himself as he will be for his author, but only his wife need know that.

Beyond pointing out the ideal, it is hard to put one's finger on exactly how an editor should behave—except that he should know what the ideal is. One of the first things young editors discover is that to some writers they will become a financial manager, confidant, psychiatrist, literary advisor, secretary and person in charge of theatre tickets, hotel bookings and restaurant reservations. Some authors are worth all this, and some aren't. Some would be worth it if they asked, but only want a distant professionalism. Knowing where and how to draw the line is the first requirement of survival, but in general it is better to do too much than too little. Gratitude is a shallow emotion, but resentment burns forever.

An editor's relationships with agents are as important as those with his authors. He should see them regularly, and will usually do so over lunch, and he should always leave them with a pretty clear idea of what he is looking for. They will tell him what they have in hand, or what may be coming, and he should know his own mind well enough to be able to tell from a description of a sentence or two whether the project is something for him. It may not be a digression to note that how a young editor handles lunch can be as important as how he handles meetings. The publishing lunch, however much decried outside of the business, serves an extremely useful function if done right. The fact that it can be nothing but an excuse for too much drink and a waste of good money does not cancel out how constructive it can be. Let us say that the editor of *Adrift* is having lunch with Callahan's agent. First the editor will bring the agent up to the minute on what is going on with that book and talk over any issues that are unresolved, say, a new advertising campaign or an as-yet-undecided reprint sale. Then the two will go over what-ever other books are in the works or just published and see if there are any problems pending with them, and finally perhaps they will discuss future projects, ideas and hopes. Along the way, trade gossip will come up—in any case friendships are formed, mutual respect estab-lished, and ambitions and abilities measured—all deposits in an account that will bear interest over the years, but which will never show up on anyone's balance sheet but their own.

In any discussion of the publishing lunch, there can be no ignoring of the general occupational hazard to which editors young and old are exposed, and that, of course, is drink. Having an important job in a large enterprise puts one in a very high pressure position. There are always too many demands on one's time and attention, and the rea-son for lunches are as much as anything to get away from meetings, the constant ringing of the telephone, and the distractions of a busy office. In any given day, the only time one ever has to focus attention on one other person, ignore all the distractions, take the time to think about complex matters, and establish positions that may well have consequences for many years later is during lunch. And so it is natural and welcome to start with a drink and then to have a glass of wine. To fail to do so is seen as being very stiff-backed indeed, and nondrinkers do find life harder than those who can manage it easily and without problem. The trouble lies with drink that becomes a problem, which is to say, when it gets out of control.

This is no place for an exhaustive treatise on alcohol and drugs and their perils, but it is perhaps worth noting that these have been problems with all too many high-powered editors and executives in the book publishing business. One supposes that matters are no different in advertising, stockbrokering, the theatre, or indeed any selling job, but a young person in publishing has to face the problem not only for himself but for how it affects his authors and his colleagues as well. The best advice, perhaps, is to remember that people with alcohol problems usually handle the matter with denial, so tolerance and a nonjudgmental attitude are necessary. No one will ever thank you for trying to reform a drunk. The only person who can reform a drunk is the drunk himself—a sad truth that all too many people forget.

In any case, an editor over time establishes himself with authors and agents both by getting to know them and by earning their respect by how he handles their business. If he is seen to be responsive, intelligent, and very much on their side when a book needs help, they will come back to him, recommend him, and offer him their own help. If he hardly ever answers the phone, never calls back, always seems to be in meetings, forgets to finish some job he has promised to do, and is generally evasive when asked direct questions, he will soon discover that all he gets to handle are things he has been assigned by his superiors, usually the most difficult and distasteful jobs around.

What is always surprising when one hears some author tell a story of how badly he was treated by his editor is how easily the editor could have satisfied the author. In case after case, one learns that what the author wanted was really something quite simple, usually only needing someone to pay attention for a few minutes or at most hours—but a long smoldering resentment has been allowed to begin because no one paid attention. Many editors make the mistake of ignoring authors' requests they don't intend to carry out instead of actually saying no. The refusal of an outlandish or unnecessary request, if done with an explanation that makes sense, is the only thing that will build respect over time. The editor, of course, must be able to sort out suggestions and requests that are actually helpful and ought to be followed up from those ideas that are mere ego building or neurotic demands for attention. As usual, tact is the key.

If the problems of dealing with authors and agents—the outside—require experience and seasoning, the problems of dealing with the inside are no less demanding, only what they require are knowledge and professionalism. For the individual editor, successful operations within his company will be carried out best when he is fully capable of dealing with the technicalities of the various skills that are exercised by the other people with whom he works. This means he must learn a lot and be aware of what other people in the firm do, how they do it, and why they choose to do what they do. Since much of what goes on inside the company is technical, there is no reason an editor cannot learn the technicalities—and he most definitely should. This may require taking courses, reading books, going to hands-on workshops, or whatever, but no editor who expects to have the respect of his colleagues should fail to consider that what he does is a craft and that he must learn the craft. The annotated bibliography and notes at the end of this book are a good place to start if one has not already learned much of what is needed.

One exercise that should not be missed by anyone seeking insight into what happens inside publishing houses is *One Book/Five Ways*. This examination of the actual internal documents of five university presses as to how they obtained, planned, designed, printed and published the very same manuscript is a classic that is, as far as I know, nowhere else duplicated. It repays close study, remembering only that since these are all university presses, what went on was much more staid and structured than is often the case in a trade house. Perhaps the atmosphere of a university press is more structured, formal and seemingly under control because it is nonprofit but does need prestige, whereas a trade house needs enthusiasm, excitement and profit, or else everybody can be out of a job. And if anyone should think that only individual people, not whole established departments, stand to lose jobs, then he or she should look into the recent history of the trade department at Harcourt Brace Jovanovich, Inc.

In successful dealing with internal matters, the young editor will have to do quite a bit of writing. Not only does he have to prepare his reports, but he also has many other tasks, including preparing the basic material about each book that may become the basis of catalog copy, jacket copy and various sales presentations. He should not let others write any of these if he can help it, because no one will know his book as well as he does, nor will they care as much about its success. We assume at this point that he will not have gotten as far as he has without the ability to write fast and well and turn out convincing copy with confidence and ease. What that means is that if he can do that, he should do it. It is a central part of his responsibility and should never be handed to anyone else.

Next is the matter of the sales conference. This fundamental ritual of the publishing house always draws the groans of the editorial staff when mentioned—and often the groans of the sales staff as well—but it has become the virtually sacred rite of every publishing enterprise, and as with meetings, it not only has to be dealt with on its open terms, but also for its informal and unstated functions.

In a typical, medium-size publishing house, there is a general sales conference twice a year. All the house salesmen as well as the independent reps attend, and the function, over several days, is for the editorial and business people to make their presentations of the books that will be published in the ensuing six months, and how they will be published. The editors present their books, jacket proofs and copy are exhibited, and advertising and promotion plans are laid out. In theory, this is the place where things are said that cannot or should not be put on paper or known outside the house—things such as how big an advance sale is expected, the quota established for each salesman, the reaction that can be expected, and whatever problems may exist. All of this varies a lot from house to house. A big house may have three or four lists a year and may break the conference up into regional divisions. A small house may do the whole thing in one morning. It doesn't really matter where the conference is, how big it is, how long it lasts, or who is there, because editorial presentations are always the heart of what happens. An editor gets up in front of the group, describes his book and talks about whatever may be pertinent. He may discuss things like advertising, and perhaps that comes later from a sales or advertising man, but what he says about a book will set the whole tone of everything that happens to it in the house from then on. In a big house, he may have rehearsed and be, in effect, reading a speech, while in a small house he most likely will speak off the cuff. That makes no great difference, because what counts is how effective he is in front of an audience that is very likely to be cynical, bored, and not inclined to believe much of what is told them.

Most editors were not trained to be public speakers, and for that reason, salesmen do not expect and, in fact, do not want an overpolished and artificial performance. Nonetheless, how good at speaking an editor may turn out to be will have a decided effect not only on his career but on the fate of his books. In former times, editors were allowed to go on and make the most obvious errors, speaking inaudibly, often at length about the plots of murder mysteries, talking while notably impaired by the drinks at lunch, or any number of other follies and horrors, but now it seems much of that has been improved and editors are either better speakers or better trained. If a young editor, then, has had no training at public speaking and shows no natural aptitude, it is time for him to seek help.

Years ago, Doubleday decided to publish what several editors thought was an extraordinarily moving book about the life of a young Jewish girl who had been hidden in an attic in Holland during the war, but who was finally discovered by the Nazis and, together with her family, was shipped off to a concentration camp, where all but her father died. It had come to the house through a contact in

140

London, and it was sort of everyone's book, as no one editor had made it his particular crusade. Each felt strongly that it should be published, but it had, for the time, a lot going against it. It was, for one thing, very much a tragedy—a downer. People like upbeat stories, inspiration, happy endings. This was the opposite, for everything in it heightened the horror and waste of what one knew from the outset was going to be a sad story. The more the young girl brimmed with life and hope and expectation, the more obscene was the awareness of her extinction. In addition, books about the war and the terrible things that had happened were becoming cloying. All the publishers lists had been jammed with war stories for years, and it seemed that absolutely everything that could possibly be said about it already had been said innumerable times. One more depressing war book? It seemed a recipe for just another forgotten publishing effort.

In spite of all this, the senior people felt that something special had to be done. The book not only had to be published, but it had to be given a more-than-the-usual chance at attracting attention. The upshot of all this was that the Doubleday sales conference was surprised one morning to see a young man who was not an editor at all step up to the speaker's table. Bill Berger had recently been hired to sell syndication rights for the Doubleday lists—excerpts from books packaged for sale to newspapers and magazines as features to appear after the book's publication. Cook books, for example, are welcome as fillers in newspaper home pages if all the editor has to do is just run it as prepared. It was a pretty new job at the time and all that anyone knew about Bill was that he was one of Doubleday's bright young men and his future would depend on what he could make of a new and untried possibility—but in any case he was in a selling job, not an editorial one, and thus was understood not to have any special attachment to the ideas of editors. He presented this book to a startled sales department, and the conviction, even rude passion that he conveyed to those assembled brought across at once that whatever it was he was talking about, it had to be something very special indeed. The book was *The Diary of Anne Frank*, which went on to become an enormous best-seller and a hit play, movie and television drama as well as a standard on college reading lists, and now is an established postwar classic which is still in print and being read thirty years later.

There are a number of points to note here. One of them is that Bill had never presented a book before and never presented one again. In fact, he left Doubleday not long thereafter to become a successful literary agent. His unique presentation carried the conviction it did because everyone there knew perfectly well that it was an almost unheard-of event. Editors do not give up the evidence of their position without a fight. One of the unspoken but revealing matters to be noted at a sales conference is who is presenting, and what is being presented—an editor's importance can be reliably gauged by the importance of his books—so for Bill, in effect, to usurp what would have been an important presentation by a senior person had to signal something extraordinary. Further, it meant that the department, for once, was acting as a group. Usually every editor is in competition with every other editor for the limited and precious amounts of attention, money and care that are parceled around among the books—but in this case everyone was chipping into one pot, and that merited a suspension of the salesman's customary disbelief.

Finally, the very roughness of the presentation itself, the lack of sophisticated polish and the obvious unfamiliarity of the speaker with the conventions of the form, were in themselves evidence that this man was saying what he was because he was passionate about it. All in all, it was very effective.

It is in its informal aspects that the sales conference is perhaps most necessary. It is an occasion for salesmen to reaffirm that they are indeed attached to a larger and living organization. Anyone who has, as I once did, traveled the small cities of Michigan, will know just how lonely and bleak a salesman's days can be. The occupational hazards of a salesman's life are drink and infidelity in addition to the regular cynicism and loneliness. After several months of talking about the same set of books day after day, a salesman is only too glad to get news of a fresh set. He needs the refreshment of sitting there being sold rather than of having to sell. He needs to tell people the truth about what he found out making his rounds—some of it good and some of it bad. He needs to have a drink at the bar with the young editors and get to know them. He needs, most of all, a reaffirmation of his belonging to a vital, capable and stable group—one that he can represent with pride and confidence.

While some of what a salesman needs can be gained from the formal sessions he attends, more will come from the informal contacts. A lot of drinking goes on at a sales conference, and with good reason. It does loosen people up, it does make them more familiar, and it does jolt them away from their daily routine. It is when friendships are formed and evaluations made, when gossip is noised about, and ideas are given a try. There are perfectly good reasons why companies sometimes insist that sales conferences be held in remote centers away from the distractions of the city—there the people who attend only have each other to talk to. It is nonetheless a somewhat dangerous practice, for it can not only be a large and unnecessary expense, but it can easily degenerate from professionalism into mere regimentation—and that is almost always a cover for weakness. When substance has given way to form, the alert will notice fear—and at that point, it is well to check the straps on one's parachute.

It seems that in almost every publishing house there is a group that is trying to either change or do away with sales conferences. As the years pass, they try different forms, different sets of people who attend, almost anything someone can think up and convince others to try. The conferences remain. The ritual is indeed necessary. Sensible management does what it can to keep conferences no longer or more elaborate than they really need be, and sensible editors learn to use the occasion for their own ends without, at the same time, annoying too many of those around them. As with any other performance, there is art to it, and to learn it requires practice, close attention and hard work. When it works, though, it can be quite exhilarating.

Perhaps one story will not be amiss. As a very young editor at Doubleday, I was assigned the task of handling the books that were published from collections of related articles that had appeared in *Fortune* magazine. The magazine would do, say, a series of twelve articles on "The Changing American Market" and then we would publish a book. They would buy a substantial edition of the book to give to their advertisers and to the trade. Whether anyone ever read either the articles or the books I never did know, but that made no difference. The *Fortune* editors satisfied their sense of self-importance, Doubleday made a profitable sale before a single copy was sold to the trade, and the promotion department at *Fortune* had an object of high seriousness to pass around. It was a bore to handle these books, not only because of the pretentiousness of their contents but because I had a secret belief that they did not sell, and if they did, they were sold to be given away to others, so no one really read them at all. When a collection came along called *The Executive Life*, I was particularly irritated. I was making seventy-five dollars a week, and although I did see how executives lived, the supposed hardships of their lives did not impress me much. I imagined that the salesmen would feel more as I did than as the executives would, so when it came time to present this book to them, I decided to let my cynical attitude show a little.

I had been trained as a public speaker from the time I was eleven and had learned to speak from a few notes. I had also done some acting and thus knew how to speak from memorized lines. The result of all that was that I made presentations from a few notes and no more. The conference was in a room jammed with perhaps eighty people, of whom about twenty-six or so were actual salesmen. It was first thing in the morning, and I knew that most of the men (they were all men in those days) had been to a party the night before and were tired, hung over and irritable. I started on my book, making some sort of crack about executives, and I got a laugh. I kept on, letting it out a little more, and soon got another laugh. At that point, I had that sudden incredible rush in the head and chest that an actor or speaker gets very rarely—I *had* these men.

I must have grinned and somehow let the intoxication show, for the sea of faces in front of me was suddenly alive, eager, openly staring at me and waiting for my next word. While I cannot now remember just what I said next, I do know that I forgot about time and just let it all out. The presentation became a performance, and I played it

145

for all the laughs it was worth. Somehow I managed to finish with a big laugh all around, and as I stood up to leave the platform, a round of applause broke out. I was astounded, and walked away trembling like a puppy. I learned later that no one had ever before been applauded for a presentation, and at the next conference I was asked to present not only my own books but those of two other editors who were nervous and inept at speaking. I wound up presenting eleven religious books in eighteen minutes—none of which I had read—thus saving the salesmen from suffering through an hour and a half of theological argument. Such are the rewards of having been trained in public speaking.

At some point during his seasoning, a young editor will realize that he lives in a political environment. Even if one is working for an autocrat as absolute and secure as the late Nat Wartels of Crown Publishers, there will still be company politics, although the matter will be muted and suppressed. The politics then will not revolve around what people think of each other, which is the usual case, but only what the autocrat himself thinks. If he takes a special interest in a young man who stays late very often because he is going through a bad divorce and hates to go home at night, then that may be viewed as just something that happened or as unconscious politics. The effect in any case is the same as in another example we have seen, of a young editor who got to know the president of his company—it was a great help in his career. They are both perhaps benign examples of politics—but politics nonetheless.

In most organizations there are two easily identifiable kinds of people—those who are into politics and those who are not. Those who are not are the people who have their jobs, do them adequately, and do not wish to have any other. A senior editor who just wants to handle his people and retire in due course is not into politics. In any organization it should be easy enough to spot the people who just want to do their jobs and be left alone. Many of them are specialists and professionals in some rather narrow range of activity upon which no one else would think to encroach. Those that are not in this position, whether they like it or not, are into politics—that is, their careers are not yet fully laid out, their ultimate job not yet defined, and their progression dependent on what others around them, both colleagues and superiors, think of them.

Some organizations are stable and people's careers within them mostly predictable, while others are subject to sudden changes and unexpected earthquakes. By definition, the most unstable are the most political, places where cliques and factions are at work promoting their own and impeding their rivals. Strong and stable management will seldom tolerate a very political atmosphere in its departments, whereas, of course, weak, uncertain, or constantly shifting management will always produce a nest of intrigue and backbiting. While these matters will be looked at more fully in the section on moneymen, since they effect any young person and his career, we must see what effect the local atmosphere may have on him.

A young person should first get a sense of just how political an atmosphere he is in. He should quietly note how long people have been in their jobs, how much they talk about each other, and how often nasty comments are made about others. If people seem mostly friendly and unafraid of each other, he should consider himself lucky, for he may just as well find that people are seething with grudges, resentments, jealousies and fears. Then he had better take care, for it is in such places that jobs change overnight, new bosses appear unexpectedly at the front door, and careers can be wounded by mere accident. In either case, the only solid position that he should adopt is one of professionalism.

It is not easy to lay out in a set of simple rules just what it means to be professional. If one tried, however, it would certainly include the following:

- Treat what you are doing as a craft and learn your craft.
- Never allow petty emotion to impair either your judgment or your performance.
- Be enthusiastic when you feel it, but never be negative.
- Maintain a decent emotional distance between yourself and your colleagues—be friendly but just the least bit formal.
- Never engage overtly in politics.
- Give the best you have regardless of whether you think it is worth it.
- Do no harm, but never compromise your principles.

If there exists a paragon of virtue and nobility who in himself has never violated any of these precepts, he will probably have the reputation of being an insufferable prig. All ideals are just that, ideals. Most of us never come very near them, but that does not mean that we should not know what the ideal is. Life is too complicated and ambiguous to live by simple rules, but people do seem to know when others are being professional and when they are not. The young person should strive at least for the ideal.

Here is a characteristic story. A middle-aged editor who has a perfectly good wife and set of children at home nonetheless falls in love with the much younger and quite glamorous art director of his department. Although they think that their romance is a secret, of course, it isn't at all. They go to lunch a couple of times a week and arrive back at the office looking starry-eyed, but this extra time away from doing their jobs isn't begrudged them at all. People know what is going on, realize that it could happen to them too, and only feel indulgent toward them. After a while, though, the other editors in the department do start to notice that their art director, who should, of course, turn her efforts toward doing all their work, is subtly being turned toward her lover's books. It seems that when she commissions assignments to do jackets from artists, she always uses well-known and even award-winning artists for her lover's books, but other editors find themselves with the work of new talents. It is not only that she is spending more money on her special friend's books, but that she is lavishing far more of her own talent on those books—to the point where other editors feel that she can't find enough time for them and pays far less attention to their needs than she should. Eventually, the slighted editors complain to their boss, because what the romance has now done is made the art director's work *unprofessional*. The executive accordingly calls the twosome in and says that he agrees that what they are doing is hurting the department and that it has to stop. The matter can be resolved in any number of ways, although it is quite common for one or both of them to leave the company, but the outcome must be that the art director spreads her talents evenly and fairly among all the editors for whom she works.

In general, it is always wrong and unprofessional to let one's emotions, no matter how strong they are, actually color one's performance and good judgment.

There are authors, for example, who are unpleasant but

nonetheless write books that make money. The ways in which people can be "unpleasant" are so varied that we cannot consider them here, but it is safe to say that every editor will have a day when he finds himself having to deal with someone he hates. All too many editors will simply refuse to deal with the author, and do all in their power to pass him on to someone else. Usually the fellow will end up being assigned to the youngest and greenest editor around, someone who is not in a position to say no. At this point, the young editor has an opportunity to either bring his editorial career alive or to enshroud it in mediocrity, for if a man is sane enough to write a publishable book, he is also sane enough to be dealt with by someone with understanding and patience. Maxwell Perkins made one of the most distinguished careers in modern American publishing history because he not only knew talent when he saw it, but also knew how to handle difficult people. Anyone who thinks he didn't have serious problems with his authors need only read *Max Perkins, Editor of Genius*, by A. Scott Berg.

If the avoidance of unpleasantness is all too common, so is the tendency to be lenient to someone one likes or feels sorry for. Urging the promotion of a colleague because he has been in a given job for too long and needs a raise is not recommended. Business promotions for sentiment are the same as social promotions in high school, and just as destructive in the long run. A man should not be promoted beyond what his abilities can handle, whether he needs more money or not. More important, the need of the employee should never come before the good of the organization. More people fail to reach executive levels because of their failure to pay attention to this point than for any other reason.

None of this is to say that ambition is bad. As long as

you are seen to be ambitious for yourself while at the same time objectively keeping the good of the company at the forefront of your calculations, then ambition will only help you along. It is when ambition becomes dangerous to those around you by your willingness to thrust others aside that it will hurt you. It may seem paradoxical, but true, to say that if you always keep the good of the company first in your mind, then you will also benefit yourself. If you are seen to be given to favoritism, to promoting your buddies, to being slightly unfair to those you dislike, then it is your own interests and your own likes and dislikes to which the company is subject. What you should be supplying is utterly objective evaluations, and the degree to which you do so will be the measure of your true competence. Within this scope, ambition which takes the form of willingly accepting new responsibilities will be welcomed.

The editor in chief may know perfectly well that you have your sights set firmly on his job, but if he is any good, he will also know that in fifteen years or so, he will be retired and someone just like you will then be ready for that job. The difference is this: Does he see you as one of his protégés, to be taught and nurtured and tested, or does he see you as an impatient young shark circling around and waiting for the first weakness to show before moving in to take an enormous bite out of his side? The editor in chief's perception is essentially political, and since he cannot but make some evaluation of the younger people around him, that is why no office is utterly free of politics.

One highly problematical area where it is now very hard to give advice is in the editor's relationship to his moneyman, or more likely, moneymen. It was always customary for the people who managed money to leave editors pretty much alone to do what they knew how to do. The editor in chief would have to meet with the moneymen and make financial projections for his department, based on what he knew about upcoming lists, but as publishing was and is so unpredictable, few took all this very seriously. My impression is that mature companies seldom allowed for smooth sailing but instead planned mostly to avoid disasters and keep things on an even keel. If a book or two suddenly took off and made piles of money, well, everyone was happy and that would be great, but the company did not then build that good fortune into the projections for the following year. That, at least, is my impression, for I know that somewhere along the line at most companies, when good things happened, they *did* start to build those things into next year's projections. Thus, Doubleday in the fifties not only expected to have a couple of best-sellers a season, they *needed* to have them or else the overhead for the whole operation would be far too big. (Overhead, and what it is and how it is arrived at, will be considered in the moneyman section). Although I am not privy to the inner councils of the companies in the field these days, I have a strong impression that the business school and conglomerational mentality has prevailed in the business, and now editors are put in the position of being expected to do next year at the least what they have done this year. We will take all this up later, but for now we must see what effect it has on the life of the individual editor.

The new practices in publishing seem to have led to the business side asking for much more prediction and a much more accurate estimate than used to be the case. I have seen editors with complicated forms which require exact book specifications, cost estimates and detailed sales projections to be filled in as a requirement for a contract. The fact that this is mostly nonsense and the figures will probably never again be looked at is never considered once the numbers have been fed into some computer. The only question we need consider here is, how does the editor deal with all this? The answer, I think, is simply to recognize that if the computer needs numbers, then give it numbers, but don't lose any sleep over giving it numbers you know yourself are entirely arbitrary. Every editor knows that to supply future numbers is mere fantasy, so the answer is to have a few reasonable fantasies at hand and fill in the blanks with one or the other of your standard models whenever asked.

At one end, take the basic minimum book that sells, say, seventy-five hundred copies at fifteen dollars. Then run the numbers for that one and perhaps three or four more up to one that sells forty thousand copies for thirty dollars. These then become your standard models, like Toyotas or Datsuns, and if you expect you have a book that may turn out to be comparable to a Grand Prix race car, just suppress that thought and predict it as another Toyota as usual. If you feed into the computer that this model is going to win at Monte Carlo and it turns out that it never even qualified to run, then the computer will eventually cough and a business school graduate will want to know what went wrong. The only way for you to win is to make modest but not wholly unreasonable projections, and to be sure to have enough material on hand at any given time to be able to substitute one book for another once you get tied to projections. That is, don't rush everything through. Don't schedule books for publication that aren't truly ready. Don't count on an author's promises of being able to finish some job on time. Don't get caught with predictions very different from what has happened in the past. Remember that moneymen produce nothing whatever themselves. They can only analyze what *has* happened, not decide what *will* happen. Above all, don't let money-men set goals for you that you know are unrealistic, for you will have embarked on a journey that ends with one or all of you looking for new jobs.

What, then, should your goals be? Should you set yourself goals at all? My answer to that is that, yes, I think it is good for a young person to have goals. Most successful editors do have what might be called a life agenda, and this seems to help them. A decent ambition is no more unseemly than a decent self-respect. Both will stabilize and give structure to a life that might otherwise be too subject to drift and a mere dumb reaction to the press of outside events. Attainable goals are an entirely worthy and honorable prospect, and you should establish them quietly for yourself when you know what is in fact realistic for you to aim for.

Standards

People who are not in the publishing business always seem to ask, "How do you choose your books? What criteria do you establish to determine what gets published? How do you know what will sell? What is your editorial policy? What are your standards?"

The most that can be said about all those questions is that they are not asked inside publishing houses because they are not relevant. The only one that ever comes up is, Do we want to publish this book, and if so why? When an editor is confronted with that specific question, he can make a list of others that need answering before arriving at a decision. The truth is that since nobody really knows what will sell or really why one book sells better than another, it is silly to try predicting, so one just relies on one's experience and instincts.

154

Years after I had been publishing—and doing so with some success—a veteran salesman, one of the most respected of his trade, said to me, "Well, you know what they say—the only things that sell books are lust, greed and local pride." It was something of a shock, because I had always thought that people bought books for all kinds of reasons—but if you were willing to add a category that might be called escape, or pure entertainment, then an amazing number of books would fall under that rubric. I did, in fact, try to analyze whole lists of books, and if all self-help and self-advancement books were bought as a result of greed, and all diet, sex, exercise, cooking, art and sundry other titles were bought to satisfy a form of lust, then, given history, biography and other local interests, what he was saying really wasn't that far off. I realized that his catchphrase meant that no one buys a book unless he feels that there is a positive benefit in doing so.

It can never be emphasized enough that each book sale is an individual act voluntarily undertaken by an uncoerced buyer. The only exception to this basic assumption has to do with books assigned in educational courses and the automatic sending of books by clubs. For this analysis, though, buying a book is and must be a positive act wherein money is given or pledged in the expectation of receiving for that money something of equal worth, judged by the buyer from the information he has at hand at the time.

Books are items of very elastic demand. There are almost none of them that you *have* to have, in the sense that a heroin addict has to have a fix, or the furnace in your house has to have oil in winter. The few books that have an inelastic demand—bibles, dictionaries, bird guides—have all long since been discovered to be in that category, and even companies that are in the business of supplying

155

those needs find that the competition is fierce. This is equally true in the textbook business—the number of books offering, say, an introduction to economics is hardly short of astounding. Publishers have neither been slow nor foolish in seeking out the lines of endeavor that offer regular and dependable sales—but just as regular and dependable sales are so highly prized, there is intense competition wherever it seems possible to achieve that result.

What editors mostly do, therefore, is to seek books for which there is little or no direct competition. Any work of art is unique. That is why editors like new novels, new stories, new interpretations, for there can be no direct competition for something that is unique. If you want a copy of *Adrift*, it is unlikely that another story will satisfy you. It may be that you would accept a new Maigret mystery if the exact one you had heard about is not available, because, after all, there are a lot of Maigret mysteries, most of them quite alike and all of a quality you find admirably high, but if you had made up your mind to read *Moby Dick*, would you settle for *Israel Potter*?

Editors read a lot. They read famous books, obscure books and manuscripts that never get published at all, and it is by constant reading over the years that their instincts mature and become reliable. An editor lives in an uncertain, shifting, confusing world in which so little is sure he may often feel that his chances of being right are hardly greater than his chances of being wrong. In the end, all that he really has is what he knows and what he feels, and the only thing worth trusting is his own deepest instinct. If, when in doubt, he calls upon his true feelings and acts upon them, he will become known as a man of integrity and as a very successful editor.

3

Moneymen in the Creative Process

IN THE PUBLISHING BUSINESS the hardest role to fill is that of the moneyman. His job is the least well understood, the least explained, and the least appreciated by others in his firm. Nonetheless the role he plays is crucial to the success of the firm, and if the function is not performed with tact, sophistication, and a long and deep understanding of the business, then it may well be poorly managed. This, unfortunately, has been the case in all too many of the firms of the modern era and is often the consequence of large corporate-style management. It is interesting to see how some conglomerates that some years ago were eager to buy successful publishing companies have lately been willing to sell them. The root cause of what must be the disappointment felt by the large holding companies is a lack of understanding of what a publishing house is and can be. The outsider naturally tends to think that publishing is a business like any other, that it can be rationalized and its growth projected along with the other disparate businesses that make up the conglomerate. This expectation and assumption is not true. Publishing is simply not like any other business.

People who look at show business, moviemaking, the rag trade, or any other enterprise that is dependent upon fashion and the popular whims of the moment—from dress designs to rock stars—all realize that there is no accounting for tastes or for fashion, and that therefore no serious businessman can expect any one of these activities to operate like a regular, ongoing business. No outsider in his right mind would think to take over a movie studio, for example. He will have heard of the vast sums that have been thrown to the winds by unseasoned executives—a vivid recent example being a movie called *Heaven's Gate*, which cost a fortune and was released unsuccessfully twice, causing a $44-million write-off and devastating the fortune of United Artists. Anyone wishing to know more about the details of this spectacular catastrophe need only read Steven Bach's *Final Cut*. No outsider would decide to back a fashion designer unless he had long and intimate acquaintance with the business. What Broadway angel expects to get his money back when he invests in a show? Yet all these businesses have, of course, made some people rich, and they must be, in some sense, a business. The point here to remember is not that the individual playwright, dress designer or rock musician need have much background or understanding of the business at all—it is that they need to be managed by somebody who does have a feel for the whole thing because he has grown up with it in his bones. It is very rare for someone who has not grown up more or less within a business to understand it well enough to run it properly, and the riskier the business the more that is true.

The trouble is that people do not think the book business is more like show business than like a manufacturing business, but it is. The most sober-sided textbook publisher, the most staid and established printer of bibles, the seemingly most entrenched and well-placed and diversified publisher is really just as subject to the whims of fashion as is a movie studio. Because this does not *seem* to be so when the business is looked at by an outsider, serious mistakes can and have been made. If one takes the income statement and balance sheet of a well-established publisher and looks at, say, its performance over the last ten years, it at once seems to be stable, predictable and rational. The outsider looks carefully at everything, talks to middle and upper management, and sees no reason why normal business practices cannot be applied to a publisher.

The trouble is that normal business practices both can and cannot be applied to a publisher, and the long-range success of the operation will depend upon someone knowing just when to be strictly businesslike and when not to be. It is not something that is easy to teach or to learn, and that is why the number of really good moneymen in the publishing business is very small—there are probably not more than half a dozen in the whole trade— and why so many of the people who have tried to fill this role either have failed outright or have done it so poorly that their function has become spread around to a group of people. The more widely decision making is dispersed, the more natural it is for it to aim at reducing risk and keeping things on an even keel. When this aim becomes paramount, the company has nowhere to go but down— and the process may take a generation or even two, but the rot is in the roots.

In this section, we shall examine as closely as can be the function of the moneyman, using that term as if it were one person, but realizing that in most present-day companies the term covers either several people or even a large group. The question is—how can the moneyman bring order and sanity to a business that at its heart is irrational?

A moneyman is the person who runs the business side of a publishing house. A couple of classic moneymanagers in recent times were Donald Klopfer with Bennett Cerf at Random House and Kurt Enoch with Victor Weybright at New American Library. In each case, the flamboyant and publicity-loving publisher acted the part of the outside man, dealing with authors, agents, the media and the public in a visible and idiosyncratic way while the moneyman shunned the spotlight but made sure that the money was properly handled and the details of running a business were neither neglected nor allowed to become too unreasonable. Both teams were highly effective and built up their houses to become major players on the national publishing scene. Today, the functions that each one of the two men in these teams managed have been broken up into parts, and the "publisher" is now most likely a whole editorial and publicity department while the "moneyman" is probably several people. For our purposes, however, we will consider that all the business side is still in the hands of one person whom we will call the moneyman.

The first thing a moneyman must understand is just what a publishing house is. Almost all publishing enterprises start as a purely entrepreneurial risk-taking business. Someone has a manuscript or perhaps nothing more than an idea, plus some money or perhaps nothing more than some credit, and causes a book to be made and put on sale. The entire sum that was spent to produce the book is put at risk, for it can be completely lost. If the entrepreneur is shrewd or perhaps lucky, however, the book proves popular and sells enough copies for the risk taker to pay off his costs and keep a profit. This assumes, of course, that the publisher is not a charitable enterprise and prices his book so that he can recover his costs from sales and make a profit, too. It also assumes that he starts with one book, although even pure entrepreneurs often start out with several. At the outset, the business is almost pure risk taking, and one of the very few examples, in fact, of a pure risk-taking enterprise in modern economic life.

In an informative article in *The New York Times* for March 23, 1986, except for the precise numbers as true now as then, Lawrence M. Fisher writes about some small and new publishers:

Berkley, Calif.—Phil Wood, founder of the Ten Speed Press here, was nonplussed when David Arora approached him with a 680-page book on mushrooms. But Mr. Wood took it home and "found myself laughing at this mushroom book that was so witty and well written. I called him the next day and said I'd publish it."

Mushrooms Demystified was a long shot even for Ten Speed, but it exemplifies the domain of small presses: Publishing books with little apparent best-seller potential that major publishers, increasingly intent on blockbusters, ignore. As it turned out, *Mushrooms Demystified* was a bit of a blockbuster itself. It sold out its original 1980 printing of 16,000 copies. While Ten Speed considers that a healthy number of copies—and in fact is about to reissue the book in a revised edition—major publishing houses ordinarily would not be interested.

Smaller presses "provide a widely diversified book press for things that are experimental, that are not geared for

161

larger markets," said Michael Bessie, a director of Harper & Row, which distributes the work of small presses. "They publish things because one person believes in them and is willing to take the risk."

There are about 16,000 publishers in the United States, of which more than 15,500 are small presses, according to John F. Baker, editor in chief of *Publishers Weekly*. "There are a lot of dropouts, people who publish one book and then disappear, never to be heard from again," Mr. Baker said. Still, he estimates 150 new publishers join the ranks each month.

No single small publisher poses much of a threat to Random House or Doubleday. As a group, however, small presses account for nearly half the sales volume of all books published and more than half the titles in print, Mr. Baker said. Further evidence of their growing impact is the rise of *Small Press,* a bi-monthly magazine published by the R. R. Bowker Company, which also puts out *Publishers Weekly,* and the growth of companies like Bookpeople, a Berkeley distributor that specializes in small publishing houses.

Many of the small houses are clustered near New York and in the San Francisco Bay area, where they benefit from proximity to each other. Ten Speed is unusual in that it handles every aspect of book production in-house, from design to warehousing. Other houses rely heavily on free-lancers, who are more likely to gravitate to an area with many potential assignments. Groups of small presses also make distributors such as Bookpeople economically feasible.

Mr. Wood, in fact, says new publishing companies have a much better chance of survival now than in the early 1970s. "There were only two or three companies in Berkeley then," he said. "Now there are forty-four publishers and two distributors." Today, he adds, "All you need is a good book. The means to get that book out to a large market rapidly are at hand."

The advent of inexpensive computers has enhanced the small publishers' efficiency, too, enabling them to handle complicated royalty systems and other bookkeeping chores in-house. Ten Speed and Inner Traditions, a small New York house, have both developed special software and sold it to other publishers.

Many small presses intentionally restrict their growth in order to maintain an intimate relationship with the books and their authors. Berkeley's North Point Press, for example, limits its list to thirty new books a year. William Turnbull, the founder, and his editor, Jack Shoemaker, expect all employees to read everything the press issues, as they do. "I like the luxury of reading everything we do, being familiar with the authors," Mr. Turnbull said.

Some publishers become almost parental toward their books, keeping them in print even if they are not selling well. "We wouldn't abandon one of our kids," said John Cassidy, thirty-six, co-founder and editor of Klutz Press in Palo Alto. Klutz, North Point and others keep their published titles in their catalogs, and sales representatives keep pushing them, rather than "remaindering" the leftover inventory to bookstores.

An active backlist is important to small presses for more than sentimental reasons, however. Many of the specialized books they publish require continued promotion over long periods of time before they catch on.

A classic example of a book that took years to find its market is the job-hunting manual *What Color Is Your Parachute?"* by Richard Bolles. Originally published by the author in 1970, it was picked up by Ten Speed in 1973, and made it to *The New York Times* best-seller list six years later, in 1979. It remained there until 1983, then returned to the list in 1985 when Ten Speed issued an updated edition. In March of 1990 the twentieth anniversary edition was number six on the *Publishers Weekly* paperback best-seller list.

A hit is helpful to any publisher's health. "Getting the

bread and butter on the table is tough in this business," Mr. Turnbull said. "We need the books that sell much more than average because we do a number of books that don't sell well at all." A successful book of poetry may only sell 2,500 copies, he said.

Although North Point and other small presses typically do not deal in best-seller material, there have been some pleasant surprises. After nearly two years in print, North Point's *West with the Night*, by Beryl Markham, an African bush pilot and contemporary of Isak Dinesen, is approaching 100,000 copies sold; it is currently the best-selling paperback in the San Francisco Bay area. *Son of the Morning Star*, a book about Custer and the Little Bighorn by Evan S. Connell, sold 120,000 copies for North Point; Harper & Row paid $210,000 for rights to reprint the book."

The article then goes on to tell of the fortunes of Ten Speed Press, founded on *Anybody's Bike Book*, and sustained by *What Color Is Your Parachute?*; Inner Traditions, which relies on the occult and esoteric; John Muir, which started with car repair manuals; North Point Press, which is a labor of love sustained by a real estate developer; and Klutz Press, which seems to have been started largely as a lark.

What is interesting about this is how much the story sounds like one that could have been written fifty or sixty years ago, only then the new firms would have been Simon & Schuster, The Viking Press, Rinehart & Co., and The Dial Press. It's as true now as it was then that new firms need a great success right at the start or else a backer with plenty of money and some patience. The Rinehart brothers were both working for Nelson Doubleday, who refused to publish a book they both thought was wonderful, so they left, formed their own company, and published *Anthony Adverse*, a great best-seller which sustained the company throughout the thirties and enabled the brothers to go on to establish a significant company. The Viking Press was started by a man who wanted to be a publisher and could afford it, having inherited a manufacturing fortune. He didn't turn a profit for ten years, but because he had both taste and integrity, the firm, once it was in the black, stayed that way for many years. Note also the fate of these four by 1986. Simon & Schuster remains one of the dominant houses in the industry, although being so now as part of a very large diversified conglomerate. Viking, after some serious upheavals, survives as the American division of Penguin. Rinehart disappeared into Holt, and The Dial Press has died entirely.

In the classic progression, a firm is started when the founder or founders are relatively young, and they usually continue to run the company during their active lifetimes. During this period, if the firm follows the normal progression, it will pass from being a pure risk-taking enterprise to one that is more stable and less subject to the vagaries of how each new list sells. This will happen as a result of the growth of the firm's backlist—those books that have already been published a given length of time, say two years, but which continue to sell. As the years go by, each new list will establish a few books as regular sellers, books which may sell for ten years or thirty years or even virtually forever. It is hard, for example, to think of when Melville, Poe, Mark Twain or Hemingway will stop being required reading for American teenagers.

My own list stands as a good example of a company that published in a conscious attempt to establish a backlist, and which did so. Clarkson N. Potter, Inc., published its first list of four books in 1960. Fifteen years later, during which time the firm had been publishing twelve to fifteen new books a year, almost half the total volume of sales for that year were generated by books that had been published at least five years before, and two thirds of sales were made by books two years old or more. If it is considered that any book that has been out two years can safely be thought of as a backlist book—and it should be—then what these figures mean for a moneyman is that for this company at that point only about a third of the firm's sales needed to come from unknown entities.

A moneyman prizes predictability almost above anything else, so the less a firm's viability depends upon the fashions of the moment and the more a regular level of backlist sales that can be relied upon, the better he sleeps. Publishing is thus a mixture of the predictable, which is the backlist, and the quite unpredictable, which is the new-books list. The mix, therefore, will depend on the kind of publishing being done. Fiction houses must learn to live with a smaller backlist than nonfiction houses. Novels may be bigger jackpots on occasion, but they don't usually have a long life. The experienced moneyman will be aware of the industry levels of the various components of his sales, and see that the house is run accordingly.

A moneyman must be aware of what stage of development a company is going through. After what might be called the establishment phase, there will be a more or less lengthy period when the owners and founders run the company, but ultimately they will retire or die, and at that point the company must be either institutionalized or passed on to competent inheritors. It is unfortunate but nonetheless true that inheritors, if they come from the founding family, seldom have the ability of the founders themselves. The list of family inheritors who failed to sustain the companies they were handed is so long and dispiriting that there is no wish to dwell on it here. Suffice it to note that founders seldom bother to train successors or consciously bring people along who will replace them, and the children of successful businessmen tend to be spared the seasoning their fathers usually endured before becoming successful. Whatever the reasons may be, the facts are that in American business generally and the book publishing business in particular, the aristocratic principle does not work. If a company is to survive well past the life of its founders, it is likely to do so only if at some point it becomes large enough and secure enough to become institutionalized.

In the eyes of the law, a corporation is a person, and this odd legal convenience happens to point to one of the central realities of any organization—that in many ways it is indeed like a person. It has a life of its own, a personality and unique character, and anyone looking at it may compare its condition to any given stage in a human life. It may seem to be a robust and healthy teenager, a complacent, middle-aged figure prone to the accumulation of fat, or perhaps a lively grandparent overseeing the growth of dynamic and well-educated grandchildren. To imagine what stage in life a company may be as compared to a person is no trivial exercise. A competent moneyman should make a well-informed judgment as to how close his company comes to being like someone he recognizes, and set his thoughts from there.

A simile, however useful, does not really cover every point in a company's life because by far the most critical transformation takes place during the process of a firm's passing from the stage where it is dominated by a founder to when it has become a large corporate organization. I call this institutionalization, and have seen it take place at Doubleday in the early fifties, and at Crown Publishers in the seventies. In both cases, an autocrat had built and run his company with a firm idea of how to make money and with no interest in other people's opinions.

In the case of Doubleday, the autocrat's death at an early age left the company in the hands of a lawyer and of managers who had survived by being yes-men. The firm could easily have gone into a gentle downward spiral, but the need for new blood was so obvious and the opportunities for new ideas so open that the people who found themselves with the company hired a number of bright young people and gave them their heads. They also let the managers of the various divisions run their sections largely as fiefs, and stayed away from them. The firm rode the postwar boom as a dynamic and forward-looking enterprise, and that kept it for a time firmly in the first rank in the business.

In the case of Crown Publishers, the autocrat did not die, but did acknowledge that he someday might, and himself supervised the training of the generation that would follow him. Nat Wartels thus presided over the institutionalizing and eventual sale of his own company, a very rare and remarkable occurrence, but one which only served to emphasize the breadth of his genius. Within the space of one working lifetime, he had taken a company that had started out at the very bottom of the Depression with a loan of $800 from his family and had seen it grow until it was one of the largest distributors of books in the country, found its books on the best-seller list as often as any other imprint, and was the basis of a fortune that made him one of the richest men in America when he sold out to Random House in 1988.

The continuing importance of Doubleday and the rise of Crown Publishers illustrate two very basic and general ideas that any moneyman must always keep in mind. The first is the durability of a well-founded publishing company, the second is the true function of the executive.

When my own children were about twelve and fourteen, I can remember that they asked me what I did all day at the office. I can also recall just how hard it was to answer that question. At one level, I could tell them that I read a lot of reports, spent a lot of time talking on the telephone about making deals concerning spending and getting money, wrote a lot of letters, attended a lot of meetings, and, basically, *decided* things for the whole company. This really didn't satisfy them, but I wasn't prepared to go to the other end of that scale, because I wouldn't have given the real answer even to another executive. The real answer was that since I had been a philosophy major in college and had taken a special interest in decision theory, I had since become a student of organizational theory in as deep a way as I could. I had found that the best, indeed almost the only, book on the subject that was at all satisfying was *The Functions of the Executive*, by Chester T. Barnard, who had been the president of the New Jersey Bell Telephone Company, one of the biggest organizations in the world. He had thought about it as deeply as the subject could go, and for anyone wanting to have a theoretical basis for executive behavior it was, then and now, what I would recommend.

Somewhere in between superficiality and philosophy, however, was practicality, and the practicality of what an executive did could be said easily enough. It was to make informed decisions such that they insure the continued good health of his company. His concern was for the whole company. At its core was confidence—confidence in employees, suppliers, customers and the outside world that his company was healthy, that it was going to be there a long time, and that it was entirely capable of carrying out not only its routine operations but whatever else it decided to do. In a well-established company with a positive cash flow, there is usually little difficulty in maintaining confidence.

Under normal circumstances, the executive is concerned with the overall health of the corpus of his company—a dynamic, living, operating entity that must have constant attention or its smooth running can go awry. Organizations have natural ills, among them being a tendency to become bloated, to lose a sense of innovation, to drift toward becoming fragmented—these among many others. The executive must always guard against these sicknesses—identify them before they become serious and extirpate them. He must keep up morale by seeing that the right people are in the right jobs, that the natural internal conflicts for the use of the firm's resources are resolved without hurt, and that the allocation of resources is as efficient as possible.

Take a simple example. In one week, the executive is told by his warehouse manager that he really needs a new warehouse, and that if the firm is to expand it will very soon be a necessity. He is told by his editor in chief that the firm has a chance to bid for the next book by a guaranteed best-selling writer, but that to get it the advance will have to be over a million dollars. And he is told by his comptroller that a very good little firm they both know about is for sale and would make a very good acquisition. Now he wants to say yes to all these people, but of course he really doesn't have the money to do so. How does he decide what to do? The answer is that he does it by using the experience of his years in the business and deciding what is most important and what comes next. He seeks advice from trusted aides and from outsiders. He works out the possible consequences of each different action. He ponders what his aims are for the company and where he wants it to be five years hence. He considers what his staff is capable of handling. He tries to think of everything, and then he announces what the course will be and tries to see that it is carried out with dispatch and vigor. Such is the daily life of the executive.

As we have seen before, the underlying durability of a book publishing company rests upon the exclusive right to print that is secured by copyright. Under the old law this period was fifty-six years from first publication and under the present law copyright runs for fifty years from the death of the author. With copyright, of course, go all rights that flow from the original publication, which may be worth far more than merely the right to print books. The firm founded by Horace Liveright, a wildly flamboyant publisher of the twenties, went bankrupt in 1933, but it had been publishing Eugene O'Neill, Maxwell Anderson and Theodore Dreiser among others, and so it lingered on until there were still things worth buying from it in 1969. A manufacturing company has no such ongoing values to keep it alive. If, for example, a printer goes under, the bank repossesses the presses which have been undoubtedly mortgaged to it, and union contracts are voided, and the stock of the company is at once worthless. There is no backlog of work that can be transferred to a new company and no residual payments may be expected. Even the plates held for possible reprints actually belong to the copyright holder and can only be used by the holder's consent. Thus a printer can and does disappear overnight. A publisher, if he has done any good books at all, can always count on some income from reprints, rights and residuals. It isn't so much that there are a lot of good books in the warehouse, it is that the warehouse stock can be indefinitely and continually replaced and renewed.

The durability of the publishing house rests further on the same thing that any large organization relies upon, which is what I have called institutionalization. This means that every function in the organization has been more or less analyzed and formalized and each job is done by a properly trained professional who is in turn training another professional to replace him in due course. An institution thus does not depend for its success upon the genius of one mind or risk failure because of the follies of an accidental decision maker. Thus not only has management been insulated from internal caprice by making decisions professionally, but it has also been freed of the whims of birth by working for an ownership which is so widely shared that it is also represented on a professional basis. Only when these two conditions have been attained can it be said that a firm may look forward to years and years of healthy existence. Institutionalization may rule out brilliance and spectacular growth, but it also is the only guarantee against gradual decline. One of the most obvious consequences that would seem to flow from these considerations is that publishers would tend to be either large formal organizations that are staid and predictable but very well established and durable or else they would be brash individual experimenters who appear and disappear with rapidity but who sometimes hit it big and manage to found small but interesting firms. This is, in fact, a good description of how publishing is in America today. The indifferently managed middle-sized firm is rapidly becoming a thing of the past.

The function of the executive is twofold. The first thing he must do, and do promptly, finally and with well informed reasons, is decide. The second thing he must do, and do well if his company is to survive, is pick his people. We shall consider each function separately.

When I was young and spent my apprenticeship at Doubleday & Co., I was able to observe that during this time the company made about seven major corporate decisions. They started Anchor Books, sold their medical textbook company, established and then abandoned a textbook division, greatly expanded and then abandoned a mass market paperback division, and closed their fifty-year-old printing plant in Garden City, Long Island. Whether they were right in these decisions could be easily debated even now, but I thought then and think now that more of these decisions were wrong than right. Did it matter to the general health of the company? Even now there is no way to tell. What it does illustrate, however, is that any executive will face, on average, a major corporate decision about once a year, and it doesn't really matter what he decides as long as he decides something. If his batting average should later turn out to be better than five hundred, then he should either consider himself lucky or be given a raise for brilliance. In the case of his daily decisions, such as the size of an advance that ought to be offered for a given book, or where to spend advertising money, or anything else, the situation is essentially the same. Since no one can ever really predict whether any given decision is right or wrong, what matters is that he decide, and that he do so in a way that satisfies those around him.

The responsible decision maker will ask for the opinions of experts, find out the thinking of his people, read whatever research reports are at hand, and become as fully informed as possible. Then, looking at what is always a sink of uncertainty, he will reach down and pull out an

173

answer. He will then know enough to never look back. The two most damaging things an executive can do is fail to execute or to fail to stand by his decision. If a decision, once made, can later be revised or even countermanded, then organizational efficiency is destroyed. The executive's word will have no standing, editors will be unable to sign up projects, outsiders will shun the company. The situation will be even worse than if the executive waits, hesitates or postpones decision making. Though delay may be damaging, it is not necessarily fatal if a decision is arrived at eventually. If a deal is not a deal, then the company needs another executive. This is not to say that a decision maker, having made a decision, cannot make another one. He should, in fact, always be ready to look again at where he is going and change when the circumstances require change. The new decision, however, must be made with the same care and thought as was the old one, and its evident need must be just as clear to those who will have to carry it out.

Sometime around 1953, Jason Epstein decided to mount a campaign in the Doubleday editorial department to get the company to publish *Lolita* by Vladimir Nabokov. It was then available in English only from La Librairie de France, the French bookstore in Rockefeller Center, where two very expensive paperback volumes could be had under the counter. It was then considered an obscene book, and whether it was actually banned or not we didn't know, but like the Henry Miller books, if the customs people found you with one in your luggage when you came back from France, they confiscated it. Jason got everybody to read it and write glowing reader's reports, and soon there was a wonderful collection of the best reports you ever saw. It was, after all, a splendid book, funny, fast, biting, sexy in an entirely innocent way, and a brilliant satirical comment

174

on American life. Of course, we were all for it and knew perfectly well that it would make a fortune if we published it.

Eventually the pressure rose high enough that Douglas Black, the president of Doubleday, called an unprecedented meeting. The whole editorial department was required to attend. At the meeting, Mr. Black explained why we would not be publishing *Lolita*. He had been one of the team of lawyers who had defended the case against Edmund Wilson's *Memoirs of Hecate County*. That book had been found obscene by a lower court and Doubleday had elected to fight the matter all the way up to the United States Supreme Court, which they had done, and where they had lost. The Supreme Court of the United States had, in effect, ruled that Wilson's book was obscene, and it was therefore officially a banned book, and Doubleday could not print it. The fight had cost the huge sum of $80,000, (around $450,000 in 1990 dollars), and Mr. Black told us that he was not about to risk the same sort of fight for any new book, no matter what its literary merit and no matter what its potential. He went on to give lawyerlike explanations for the various arguments and to deliver a lecture on what constituted obscenity in the eyes of the law. We were all quite disappointed, and were later irritated to see the book published by Putnam.

Putnam never spent a nickel defending it in court. It became a huge best-seller, revitalizing a company that was at the time in questionable shape. What might it matter that Putnam's decision may have been made on the most trivial ground? It gave the whole company a tremendous lift. And what did it matter to Doubleday? Did it hurt the company to lose so big a winner? It would probably later judge that it was so big that one book could not make that much difference and that as a company it wasn't hurt. My feeling, however, is quite different, and I think now that it did indeed hurt the company. Nabokov went on to be a truly major figure, but he always kept the reputation of writing literature. He was able to write books that were commercial successes while at the same time satisfying the needs of the people of High Seriousness—the kind who would later write for *The New York Review of Books*, and who then and now write for the quarterly magazines, and the academic journals—people who took most popular novelists as being beneath contempt. Nabokov was always taken to be very highbrow, and if he had been on the Doubleday list for the years after *Lolita*, his name alone would have saved the company from being regarded—as it was and still is—as an irredeemably lower middlebrow house.

Does any of this ever show up on a balance sheet? No. Should a good publishing moneyman be aware of these subtleties? Yes.

After prompt and firm decision making, the most important thing a moneyman or chief executive can do is pick the people around him who do the jobs that count. He should select the people who are next beneath him in the hierarchy, most probably all the department heads. These will be editorial, sales, production, advertising and promotion, and of course his own people in the accounts and royalty departments. Different companies are organized quite differently, but what counts is that each job has a clear area of responsibility and a clear idea of who is in charge of what. Advertising, for example, is often a matter of competing interests as between the sales and editorial departments. The sales department wants to spend the money on its blockbusters while the editorial department wants to use more of the money for getting lesser books noticed. Who decides how the spending is done? It hardly matters what the answer is as long as there is a clear answer, and someone who is definitely in charge of such decisions.

The art of choosing the appropriate person to fill a given job is nowhere written down as a set of rules but may fairly be said to come down to questions of competence and character. For many jobs, there are candidates who are young and working up to more responsibility, and so it becomes a case of picking from among established candidates. Both top editors and sales managers are likely to have come up through their departments, and the same may be true in art, production and the others. If a company has to go outside, then the usual resumes and recommendations are guides, but even they are not always reliable. In any case, it is usually possible to establish someone's competence by using some objective standards.

Most good executives are able to judge how well a given person should do in a job and also how he is doing his job once he has it because at one point they did the job themselves. Most can be learned in a year or two, so if the executive has done some job for that long he is pretty sure to be able to tell how someone else will do in it. That is why good moneymen usually have grown up in the business and why publishing people are very suspicious of people who have learned what they know at some other kind of business and expect that general knowledge can be applied to publishing. It is not that the vagaries and hazards of publishing are unmanageable, it is that they are best managed by people who are used to them.

The problem, of course, comes when the executive tries to hire people for jobs he himself hasn't done and doesn't understand. The purest example of this difficulty can be seen in the history of Nat Wartels's relationships with his editors. One way or another, Nat had done just about everything in his business himself and could not be fooled in any of those areas. He had never, however, tried to be an editor, and really had no idea of what editors did all day or what went on in their minds. All he knew was what the results were when he followed their recommendations, and the results were invariably disappointing. Things simply did not go as editors said they would. They would fail to tell him when he had a big seller on his hands so that he would conclude it was a result of the efforts of his sales and promotion people. Sales and promotion would also predict great things for books that got well reviewed but never sold. Since, for Nat, money was the only criterion of success, he felt that an editor's attempts to win respectability were an incomprehensible waste, never seeing that the editor thought respectability, once established, would turn into money in due course. Nat did not see that connection, and for that reason, among others, he wasted the talents of more good editors than anyone else in town. One need only read Hiram Haydn's memoirs to get a sense of how Nat and his editors were forever at odds. In the end, the only people who could stay with him any length of time were the ones who could invoke the ultimate American justification—it makes money, doesn't it? They knew enough to never tell him what they were doing or why they were doing it, and he learned never to ask.

What this means is that if any moneyman is faced with the task of picking a chief editor, he is best advised to let another editor do the picking. Thus an editor in chief should pick his successor, and it should preferably be someone he has worked with for some time. The only exception, of course, would come if the moneyman himself had extensive experience as an editor. If all else fails, the moneyman should listen closely to trade gossip, for the ranks of senior editors are small. Sooner or later, everybody gets to know everybody else, and after a few years an editor gets a reputation. This is especially the case when someone has held a job at two or more houses, and there is no reason not to listen to what is on the wind.

If there are reasonably objective ways to assess a person's competence, the same cannot be said for the judgment of character. There it comes down to an executive being able to judge another person's inner strength or weakness, but that judgment depends on the inner strength of the executive himself.

During the Watergate mess in Washington, a wise old judge from the South was asked what he thought about it all. He said that looking at the people in the Nixon administration made him wish that there was a law saying that no one could enter the front door of the White House unless they were at least forty years old and had suffered a major disappointment in life. It was a remark that did not get much notice at the time, but it is a very good offhand way to sketch what a person of character might be.

Here we must consider five talents that some people have in abundance and some not at all, but which are crucial to success in life as well as in business and which are not taught, not measured, but gained largely out of the awareness of most people most of the time. Perhaps, taken together, they could be called a constellation of talents or even mere facets of one underlying talent. For this discussion I shall consider them and try to explain them as if they were each a separate entity which can be considered and judged by someone knowledgeable.

The first talent is politics. It has been said by many far more experienced than I that a good politician can go through a room full of people, shaking hands and talking to each person in turn and exchanging a few sentences and at the end have a clear and accurate idea of who each person is and what his capabilities and ambitions are. This ability to size people up very quickly, to judge their potential for usefulness and for loyalty with almost no mistake, is a rare and precious talent. It often goes with deep underlying insecurities, and appears to be entirely instinctive. It is said that Lyndon Johnson was a master at it, and it was obvious that Mayor Ed Koch was not very good at it. Some of it is expressed in the proverbial "woman's instinct" and some of it is exemplified in the political boss: Boss Tweed, Carmine DeSapio, Richard Daley, or Franklin Roosevelt. It is not in their ability to manipulate others that these people are remarkable, but in to knowing just how far someone else is capable of going. Although some people with natural political talent do get elected to public office, the really shrewd politicians seldom make much public show. They don't have to, since they are effective by being out of sight, and as they are blocking careers as well as promoting them, who needs publicity? The talent is in seeing to it that people find themselves in slots where they are effective and feel both productive and comfortable. Every large organization needs people who can make those determinations because one that has too many people in the wrong jobs will be a misery to everyone.

The second talent is what I term diplomacy. This is the ability to cut through what people are saying and know what they actually want. It is called "uncovering the hidden agenda" by the social scientists who have just discovered it, but it is what any seasoned diplomat should be able to do. Is someone talking in a meeting about doing something and making an argument for it on its merits or for some other reason? When opinions are formed, who is being listened to? Is the person a follower of someone else's lead? What interest is uppermost in his mind? What are his true motives? Some people spend their whole lives believing everything that they are told and some imprison themselves in cocoons of imagined conspiracies, but most of us manage by retaining an ever-ready skepticism and trying to discern the truth that other people very often wish to hide from us. The talent implies more than just the ability to cut through to true motives; it means being able to avoid intimidating others with your knowledge. People dissemble for a reason. You must know enough to deal with them on the overt level and the masked level as well, and this is what diplomacy has always been all about. As with the other talents, it seems to be mostly natural and rather rare. More than the others, it appears to be teachable. People who put their minds to it do seem to be able to learn how to be a reasonably good diplomat. Much lies in discretion, and that can be brought into conscious control.

The third talent is leadership. So much has been written about it that we shall not go over all that ground here. We will note, however, that American culture, egalitarian and democratic as it is, expects and allows for leaders to rise naturally from anywhere. Oddly enough, few politicians or generals are natural leaders, although the greatest of them certainly have been. History is largely a record of the doings of great leaders, but effective leadership is a necessity to the success of any large organization and is needed even in a very small enterprise. We all know that in any group of people there may be one or two who just naturally seem to stand forward, whom others are willing to follow. The question one must ask, then, in thinking about someone is whether he is a leader or a follower. Most, of course, will be followers, but some more slavish than others, and some unable to join a group at all. In addition, leadership sometimes does not show up until a

181

person is no longer young, being the product of experience and seasoning. In any case, it is a well-known quality, much examined, and with a large literature. We only need note that it is as important in a business organization as it is anywhere else.

The fourth talent is teaching. Being able to teach is as natural and as rare as is leadership. Being willing to teach is no guarantee to its effectiveness, and, for reasons I have never understood, practice at it seldom makes for improvement. Unhappy as the conclusion may be, it does seem that good teachers are born and not made. Teaching, however, is crucial to the successful transfer of knowledge and skill from generation to generation, and without it an organization will slowly wither and die. That learning takes place constantly is an absolute necessity for any organization that intends to last. For this reason, it must prize its teachers and encourage them, and thus many organizations will keep people who are marginal in all other respects if they are good teachers. As everyone knows, a good one is often not actually the best at what he is teaching, but everyone also knows that this does not matter. My most effective teacher was an alcoholic, but I learned more from him than I did from all the other hot operators around me. As with leadership, there is a considerable literature on teaching, so we need not dwell on it, but it is well to discover who can teach and who can't.

The fifth talent is salesmanship. We all know what that is, don't we? It's the talent that lets a man talk an Eskimo into buying the proverbial refrigerator or gets you to feel good driving away from the used-car lot in a crate that is going to expire the very day the warranty runs out. That, of course, is one image of the salesman, the fast-talking hustler who peddles shoddy goods as if they were made of solid gold. But this is only one image of the salesman.

What is meant by salesmanship in the book business and in any one where what is being sold is actually something of value is the ability of the seller to convey the underlying values and to encourage the buyer to go just a little further into the unknown than he might venture by himself. True salesmanship does not imply selling false values, but lies instead in realizing actual values.

Salesmen, like teachers, are born. The good ones have a certain likability or believability that allows them to comfortably engage other people's attention and enables them to put forth ideas that are both acceptable and useful. Some people exude hypocrisy, others betray cynicism, and many exhibit conscious manipulation—and none of these will be successful salesmen. In the book business as in almost any serious business, a good salesman is amiable, low-key, well informed, and aware of both the needs his customers and the wants of his company. In publishing, a salesman must live with the knowledge that all books are returnable, so if he overloads someone with his product, it is just going to come back. He must also keep in mind that he himself will be back. Selling is not a one-shot matter, but a question of a long-term working relationship with people who are mutually dependent, and his function is just as much to avoid having a buyer become overenthusiastic about a book that won't sell as it is making sure he has enough copies of a book that will sell. In any case, an unaffected openness and a practiced and professional understanding of books are what make a good salesman. Like any talent, people have it in varying degrees, and like looks, it can be changed only within close margins.

These various talents are distributed most unevenly, and for anyone to have even one of them in abundance is rare. A moneyman must be on a constant lookout for them, though, for when he finds someone with a lot of one or more of these talents he has someone exceptional and someone with an unlimited future. It is important to note that because most of these talents cannot be taught, they do not figure in any way in formal schooling. As far as the academic world is concerned, these talents do not exist, and if they do, they don't matter. They do not turn up on a single one of the tests that a student has taken. The young person will be largely unaware of his own abilities in any of these directions and will almost never understand that his academic success is as largely irrelevant to a businessman as his real talents were uninteresting to his college teachers. His success in business, however, will depend far more on his native talents than on anything he learned in school. This is not to say that formal education is a waste or that great success at it is of no consequence. It is rather to point out that education, however necessary and useful, is only a part of life. A mature moneyman is never going to ignore a young person's success in school, but is just going to use it as one of many criteria that interest him.

Besides talent, or even a number of talents, what helps a young person most is drive, an inner wellspring of energy that seems to be always turned on, and which is not scattered and wasted but tends to be directed to a definite goal. Some people have huge amounts of energy but are always changing the focus of what they direct that energy toward. Others are workaholics but seem to have no special goal except that of doing the work itself. A person with drive may not seem to have such an abundance of energy, and may not strike others as a compulsive worker, but he will have that most important quality of staying power—the strong positive push toward his goal that never is turned aside, never abandoned, but pursued with an assured determination until its end is realized. It has been noticed often enough that the heads of some of our largest corporations are frequently people with quite ordinary and unspectacular youths, people who succeeded because of their drive rather than any great brilliance. Someone with an overrevved drive can be an exhaustion and an irritation to anyone near him, so no matter how great someone's drive is, it must be moderated by control and consideration. Most people get tired enough just keeping up with their jobs, so the man with energy to burn should take care not to singe others with it.

The most elusive and probably least formed part of a young person is his character. By character I mean the inner strength to meet adversity and overcome it, and the ability to grow in response to a challenge or to increased responsibility. Harry Truman is generally regarded as a man who grew greatly as his responsibilities suddenly enlarged almost beyond thinking. The depth of his nature had never been tested in the extreme until he assumed the presidency and had to make the fateful decision about the atomic bomb—but he proved equal to the demand and is now understood to have been a man of great character. The same cannot be said of the men around Richard Nixon, most of whom behaved like guilty children when stressed. The Victorians seemed to think that hardship formed character—only they meant physical hardship. My father thought that hard work, meaning sweaty labor, was good for me, never thinking that hard work is just hard work and mostly unpleasant. Hard work, unfortunately, merely grinds people down. Genuine hardship on the other hand is accepting responsibility and living with the consequences of making a mistake. That does build character. Dealing with the results of what you yourself have chosen is the beginning of character. Whether it may be

185

discerned in a young person is problematical—but a wise moneyman will consider the possibility of its emerging in due course. If he does see it, he should nurture it, for in doing so he may be grooming his own successor.

Here it is necessary to go into some of the details of the balance sheet in ways that will point out the special differences one finds in a publisher's accounts compared to other kinds of businesses. For the purposes of this discussion, we will assume that the reader is familiar with normal business reporting and accounting, so we will not go into those details. We will bring up only what seem like the most important oddities one should understand when thinking of a publisher's condition.

Perhaps the most fundamental subject is royalties. Royalties are the monies that the publisher pays the author for the right to print and sell his work. They are almost always calculated as a percentage of either the retail price—the official selling price of the book at retail—or the net price—the actual amount of cash that the publisher gets per copy. Royalties may typically be 10 percent of the retail price of every copy sold of a hardcover book and 5 or 6 percent of a paperback. At the outset, it is best to understand that royalties are a complex matter and of the greatest importance to both author and publisher. The percentages that are mentioned in the contract may usually obtain, but nothing about royalties is written in stone, and the most serious negotiations in the whole course of publishing will be over just what the percentages may actually be. Royalty rates are by far the most important matter fixed by an original contract, for both author and publisher must thereafter live with whatever has been signed. In rare cases, the rates are changed later, but that is most unusual

186

and generally leads to an unsatisfactory outcome for one side or the other.

Obviously the fact of royalties tends to make author and publisher partners in the selling enterprise, for, naturally, poor sales hurt both and better sales help both. For this reason, it is well if both sides feel that the royalty rates are "fair." "Fairness" is usually determined by how close the parties think they are to the general trade average. The result of these feelings is that royalty rates do in fact appear to be quite uniform throughout the industry, even though the various percentages may seem to an outsider to be both complicated and arbitrary. Nonetheless, we may take for this discussion that in the typical novel, for example, the royalty rate will be 10 percent of the retail price. On a twenty-dollar book, the author gets a royalty of two dollars a copy—but he only gets the money after the publisher has actually collected it, and he only gets it after it had accumulated for a six-month period, both details of great importance which we will look into more carefully later.

The point to notice here is that if a publisher is paying the author the normal rate on a novel, since he gets on average 54 percent of the retail price of the book, he will be actually paying out in royalties just under 19 percent of all the money that comes in. Publishers have different discount schedules, but they are all sliding scales of discounts for the different kind of buyer—small store, library, wholesaler, large chain, and the like—all designed to encourage bulk buying and thus dependent upon volume for the precise discount rate for any given order. Better minds than mine have calculated that the overall industry average of discount comes to 46 percent, which is why I have said that on average a publisher actually gets 54 percent of the stated retail price on sales of regular hardcover books.

In terms of percentages, then, royalties are one of the biggest components of a publisher's accounts payable, and it thus behooves us to understand them somewhat more deeply.

It is best to start with advances, for this is where the author, agent and publisher will always start themselves. When a contract is made, a publisher almost invariably hands the author a sum of money as an "advance." This is an amount of money that is given to the author "as an advance against royalties." What that means is that the publisher sets up an author's account into which all his royalties will go from sales of books, rights, or whatever else comes in, and trusting that this will have a positive balance as soon as the book is published, he gives the author some portion of that expected take before it actually comes in. Thus, in theory, what the author gets is his own money, but it is money that he is only expected to earn later. When the book is published and as it continues to sell, monies accumulate in the author's account. When enough has accumulated to repay the publisher what he has already laid out, then there is a true positive balance in the account and he starts to pay out in six-month intervals as much as has been earned in the period, less a reasonable reserve for returns.

The historical reasons for a publisher giving out an advance lay in the circumstance that when a contract was signed the book was seldom finished and the author badly needed money. The classic reason a publisher gave an advance was to enable the author to finish the book. To this day this reason is valid, and it certainly will be so in the future. Authors indeed are often poor and indeed need something to live on in order to be able to finish a book. Nowadays, though, the number of advances that are made for that reason may be one in ten. The majority are paid for other reasons. And what are they? Mostly so that the author's ego is stroked and publisher exhibits a certain level of commitment to a book. The higher the advance, the greater the stake in the book the publisher will have and thus the more he is likely to try and get his money back by making a big selling effort. Agents therefore always press for the biggest advance they can get, but they also, of course, press because everybody would rather have money now than wait something like a year for it.

The typical amount of time between the signing of a contract and the first accounting for royalties may be around eighteen months, and is often much more. Even if a manuscript is ready for the copy editor when it is delivered, it takes six months to publish, and then most of another six months before the first statement is due. The *shortest* period between signing and further payment, then, is likely to be at least a year. Clearly an author wants to see something for his pains when he signs a contract even if there is no further work to do. The press for an advance is much more urgent if there is still work needed.

But just what is an advance? To an author, it is an outright payment; to a publisher, it is a loan let out at no interest, and to an accountant, it is a corporate asset. Each view must be examined.

Most authors and most agents view advances as outright payments from a publisher that are, in effect, guarantees. They do not look at the monies as loans and do not think that they must repay the sums outstanding if their book doesn't make enough money to cover the advance. In this they are wrong technically, but they are right in practice. The wording of most contracts provides for the advance to be repaid from all earnings under the contract, but most authors and agents interpret this to mean that an

189

advance is to be repaid *only* from earnings under the contract. It has happened all too often that an enthusiastic publisher has given out a large advance, received a poor book or maybe just an unpopular one, and then published it to discover that earnings nowhere near covered what he laid out.

For years it has been doctrine that publishers would not let go of their *theoretical* ability to claim the advance back but would never in practice go to court over the matter. It was thought that a public suit for the recovery of an advance would so sour all agents and all other authors on that publisher that he wouldn't be able to compete. It seemed that the spectacle of a large, well-established company suing a single poor author would generate such bad publicity that such a fight would be self-defeating. Thus an advance was really a guarantee and really non-returnable, only publishers thought it best not to admit that. They wanted to reserve the right to sue even if they never actually did so. The only exception to the general nonreturnability of an advance would come up when a book, contracted for and upon which part of an advance had been paid, turned out to be something the publisher didn't want to go ahead with once the whole book was finished. Since most books are contracted for long before they are completely finished and often before much more than an outline is available, nasty surprises do turn up. The publisher may decide that the book he finally gets isn't what he thought it would be, or he may decide that he doesn't want to do that kind of book after all, or he may have fired the editor who signed it up to begin with. Whatever his reasons may be, he makes up his own mind, and the author usually cannot change it.

Quite often the publisher decides he does not want to go ahead on a book that is, in fact, perfectly publishable.

Some other publisher would be happy to take it on. At that point, the first publisher will ask for the return of his original advance from the one paid by the new publisher. There is a certain fraternity among publishers, and they all have an interest in upholding the principle that advances are loans to be repaid, so one publisher will always compensate another when these cases turn up. If a publisher feels very hesitant about suing an author, he would not have the same inhibitions when it comes to a rival. Since an author loses nothing by these arrangements, but does get to see a book published that might not be, he will invariably go along.

In many cases, however, a book that seems unpublishable to the publisher who let the contract in the first place will seem equally unattractive to other publishers, and so the project just expires. The author is often not good for the advance even if he were to be sued and can't find another book with which to fulfill his obligation, if he feels any, so there is nothing for the publisher to do but write it off.

To a publisher, an advance is a bet on a future outcome, and a loan made at no interest. It ties up his capital, puts very large sums as risk, and binds him into the publication of a book that he may or may not really want when it is finally delivered. Obviously he should try keeping the total amount of money he has out in advances as low as possible, and almost all publishers do attempt to avoid large advances, especially ones that may be out for any length of time. Advances are typically paid in parts, some on signing, some on delivery of the manuscript, and some on publication. The closer the publisher can come to laying his money out just before he starts getting it back, the better he is at managing his money. He will try hard to avoid advances that are actually paid out before he has a complete manuscript. That is bad business practice and bad psychology—for an author needs the promise of a payment to spur him to the completion of his book. A payment that is delayed until delivery, then, serves two purposes—it encourages the author and it shortens the time the publisher has his capital out.

While a good publisher will want to keep his total of advances paid out a reasonable figure, he will also know that without a certain number of contracts and advances out, he will not have a list to publish. An advance is a claim on a work that is very strong, and having advances out and authors working on contracts are his only guarantee that he will be able to present a new list each season. While I do not know if the moneymen in other houses do this calculation, I do know that for many years I had an average of forty to fifty contracts that were out, signed, and in work at a time that I expected to publish around fifteen books a year. Since it is so hard to tell just when a given book will really be ready, it is necessary to have more contracts out than you expect books coming in. Also, a certain number of contracts don't work out. The author dies, or is lured away to do something else and never gets around to finishing your project, or any one of dozens of other difficulties arise. In those cases, you either forget the contract or put it on the back burner. I have had to wait ten years or more for a book to be ready from the time I made the first contract for it, and I know that is not considered too unusual. In any case, contracts should be made at roughly the rate that books are published, and the cushion in the middle should not be any fatter than need be.

Two special cases are worthy of note. The first is the truly huge advance. It will happen on occasion that an agent will have a very big author or a very big book and will put the matter out on auction. In this case, the advance becomes the price the publisher must pay to get the book in the first place. These games are played all the time, but they are games for only the most knowledgeable and sophisticated of players. The payoffs can be huge, but the risks are huge also. All that can be said about such things in general is that the editors and moneymen who do get into such games should insist upon knowing as much as possible about what it is they are bidding on, and should not bid beyond the capability of their firm to suffer a considerable loss. Some bids that seemed daring at the time paid off tremendously, but others went completely sour.

Perhaps at this point a digression will not be amiss, for many readers may well be aware that during the 1980s, some authors were getting huge advances—advances so big that they became news stories in the daily papers. Two questions arise from that. First, how come that happened? Second, did such advances represent a new reality based on rational expectations or were they often not earned back?

There seems to be two reasons for huge advances. The first is imbedded in how some people have been thinking about "lead books" for some time—namely that a good big house needs a lead book. This has a solid basis in merchandising theory, and used to be much on everyone's mind during the early paperback wars over rack space. Since the paperback publishers knew that only those books that got displayed in racks could be sold, there was intense competition for rack space. The publishers felt that they had to have a "leader" each month—a book so attractive that the store with the racks would feel that it had to display that one book. With it, of course, came the rest of the publisher's books for the period, so having a lead book pulled the whole list along with it. Therefore, if the publisher had paid a little too much in an advance to get that lead book, whatever it failed to earn back as an advance was money that they had actually contributed to promotion of the whole list, and it was worth the cost on that ground.

This theory of the loss leader, of course, is why discounters advertise best-sellers with a cut price. The idea is to bring in the customers with an attractive price for a very popular book, and hope that a lot of people will buy something else as long as they are there. This actually works fine, but all retailers operate on such a thin profit margin that it is a hazardous ploy and only successful for a limited time and when in the hands of professionals. The list of failed discounters is too long to include here, but it did turn out that Crazy Eddie was, in fact, crazy if he thought he could go on offering the deals he had been offering. The same is true of book discounters. They can stand to do it for a few top best-sellers on the theory of the loss leader, but they can't do it for everything in the store.

The same kind of thinking seems to still pervade the larger publishers. Top publishers should have top books, so to reach out with a lot of money for what will be one of the biggest books of its season—or perhaps they think it will be *the* biggest book of its season—is to insure that the whole list is exciting and acceptable. There may, in fact, be something in this idea, for I well remember gatherings of sales manager of several different houses who thought that the entire retail business, especially at Christmas, was affected by whether or not the business as a whole had a book that brought in people who did not usually go into bookstores. In the year that *Death of a President* by William Manchester was published, the first big book about the Kennedy assassination that had enjoyed the cooperation of the family, it was bought and read by large numbers of people who never usually thought about buying a hard-cover book. Thus it was a leader for the whole industry. It seems to me that least some of the justification for some of the very big advances of the eighties lies in these ideas. What is probably much more important, though, is the politics within large organizations and the egos of those people who run them.

Two effects seem especially important here. The first comes from a young editor on the fast track to the executive suite. A shrewd agent spots a young goer and offers him a big author or book. Now a youthful career is helped along wonderfully by being the editor of huge, expensive best-sellers. Once the young editor then is enlisted as a partisan for an expensive book, he will have good reason to push as hard as possible for it, and does so. At that point, the head man must become involved, and at the level of the big players, there are really no more than a dozen or so in town who can be in the game. If the young editor is able to enlist the competitive instincts of the boss in his quest for the big-time deal, then it may soon become the same as in any auction where two or three people decide that they must have the same thing—the price can go through the roof. It seems to me that this was going on quite regularly during the eighties, carefully orchestrated by agents who were as tough as they were smart.

It has to be remembered that one of the consequences of all the corporate mergers in publishing has been that there are a number of really big companies in the business now, some backed by even bigger outfits. This gives the people who run a big company access to very large sums of money if they think they need it—and something that can be done will often actually be done simply because the money is at hand. Power unused is no power. Power used is demonstration of its scope. The egos of the chief executives of these corporations are all large enough to have gotten them to the top in a highly competitive game, and if an agent or a young editor can stimulate their juices, the game can suddenly get expensive indeed.

The shakeout, of course, has already taken place. The books often didn't produce even a small percentage of what they needed to make in order to earn back the outsized advances. In early 1990, S. I. Newhouse, one of the owners of the Random House group, told some friends at a cocktail party that he had just written off almost a million dollars on a single book. The firm had advanced that much to get the book, and when it was published, it earned about sixty thousand, leaving a deficit in that account of nine hundred and forty thousand, not to mention the wasted advertising that was run to try recouping the advance. Random House, now privately owned by the Newhouse family, doesn't divulge its figures, but no publishing house can write off a million dollars on a regular basis and stay profitable, and one can be quite confident that Mr. Newhouse knows that. Simon & Schuster had announced late in 1989 that it was taking a $140 million tax write-off in that year. They did not specify why, but the loss was probably due largely to unearned advances as well as unexpectedly large returns of books from the booksellers. The big outfits may feel a relentless pressure to publish best-sellers, but foolish risks are still foolish risks.

In any case, the moneyman should be concerned with how long the money will be out as much as how big the amount is. He must also be able to calculate the size of the possible payoff if his most optimistic scenario is realized— that is, calculate the nature of the risk on the good side as well as the bad.

The other case is the house that has almost no advances

out. I was actually involved with one well-established publishing house that turned out not to have any advances out. The proprietor thought that he was a good, cautious and shrewd operator by not having any of his money tied up in advances—but I thought that any outfit that had no advances out was likely to get few books of any kind in and none of great note, and so what that information really signaled was that the firm was moribund. Since he is in a risk-taking business, a publisher who is taking no risks must be doing nothing interesting. It turned, out, unhappily, that I was right and the firm has now disappeared.

To an accountant, a publisher's advances are assets on his balance sheet. They are monies that he expects to get back, and from an accounting point of view, they are just like Citibank loans to Brazil—corporate assets. The fact that things are more complicated than that doesn't concern him at all. They are assets until they are declared to be uncollectable, and then they are written off. Unlike a bank, which can put certain loans in a nonperforming category when interest payments are either late or inadequate, the publisher, who does not charge interest, can only have an advance carried either as good or not good. An outsider looking at a publisher's balance sheet and the publisher's own moneyman both should know that the simple figure listed as advances outstanding needs careful analysis before they can make some kind of judgment as to just how real that figure may be. What most publishing houses do is review from time to time—at least once a year—all outstanding contracts. Each editor gets a list of his outstanding contracts and is asked for a status report on them. Then the publisher's accounts department has considerable leeway in deciding how much they do or do not want to write off. A publisher with a big profit who

197

wants to have his profits reduced to lower his tax burden may write off a lot, while another house that wants its balance sheet to look strong will just carry everything along.

A few years ago, there was trade gossip in New York that a certain publisher had suddenly and quite uncharacteristically started to sign up very big books by offering huge advances to authors and agents. Surprisingly, this went on for some months, and then it was announced that the firm was being sold, and the whole thing made sense. All those big recent advances went right on the balance sheet as assets, and so the price of the company as a whole reflected these "assets" when it was sold. It seemed a pretty transparent maneuver, but apparently it worked.

A moneyman, then, will want to know several things about his advances outstanding. First, how old are they? Second, how good are they? That is, will we get a book at all? Third, what are the chances that when the book in question does come in it will earn back its advance? When he thus has an informed estimate from his editors, he can then make the necessary adjustments in his own mind, because his fourth question is going to be, what is the total amount out in all advances? He will note that every time a book is published, an advance stops being an advance and is simply part of an author's royalty record, and every time his editors make a new contract, they will lay out an advance, so that at any given time he will have a "float" of money outstanding in his advances account. He should know what that total is and whether it is stable. He should also remember that although the accountant lists it as an asset, he (the moneyman) must think of it as a liability, for all of it can be lost, and no interest is being earned on it while it is an advance.

We now turn to the question of royalties that have been

collected and are owed to authors. Here the accountant lists payments due to authors as liabilities to the firm—just another set of accounts payable. But it isn't that simple. The only sense in which royalties are ordinary accounts payable is on the occasion of a bankruptcy, when an author indeed is merely one more unsecured creditor. In a merger or a sale, however, author's accounts must be paid up and current, for all contracts may be abrogated if royalties due have not been paid in full. Authors' royalties are thus by no means just another account payable, but a very large portion of all the money that a company owes, with a privileged standing as being central to the existence and the good name of the firm.

We must now consider the practical effect of the publisher's practice of paying his royalties at six-month intervals. Let us say that he pays on the first of January and the first of July. We will leave aside several matters that are necessary to adjust for in reality—that accounts are reckoned as having closed four months before payment, that the book business is highly seasonal, and that cash collections from sales take an average of ninety days to come in. For our purposes, let's just assume that what is due gets paid up to date in full. This means that in the first weeks of January, the publisher collects a certain amount of money that he will later have to pay out in royalties, and as the weeks go by, each individual author's account builds up money until at the end of June a check is made out for the whole amount, thus bringing that account down to zero again and starting the next six-month cycle. The upward accumulation of money in each account may be irregular, but if the publisher takes all his accounts together, the curve will smooth out, and he will be acting as a banker for the royalty money that has come in until he has to pay it out. He thus has a float just as a bank has. If he arranges for his royalty statements to go out on a monthly basis, such that on any given month he is paying one-sixth of the total, then the rest of the money is a float for that month, and in fact, he has five-sixths of the money he owes in royalties as a permanent revolving float.

It should be noticed that the actual amount of the float will be in theory just half of the amount that accumulates in each account from the first day of the period to the last day. The float should be on average just half of all the money that is paid out in each six-month period. This is what balances his advances, for this money is in fact a loan made to him by his authors, and it carries no interest payment, no more than an advance does. Unpaid royalties are thus in fact a huge asset to a publisher because they are in fact working capital that he can use without paying interest on it. The fact that they show up on his balance sheet as a liability is just as much an accounting fiction as is carrying advances as assets. The reality is that the larger the royalty due account, the bigger the publisher's float. A good moneyman will know the total size of this account and the total size of his float just as he will know the total of his advances, and one may suppose that he will consider it prudent that his float should always be bigger than the total of his advances.

If that seems complicated, it is only the beginning. To understand modern publishing, it is necessary to go a couple of steps further. There have been some exceptions to the normal way royalties are paid, and since they have changed the whole nature of some publishing houses, it is worth knowing how and why this happened.

In the middle fifties, the best-seller of its day was *The Caine Mutiny*. This was just what its author, Herman Wouk, had expected, and so, in a clever ploy, he had signed in his original contract a clause that Doubleday would pay him no more than $25,000 a year. He knew that books make money all at once, that royalties are regarded as ordinary income, and that he would face what he regarded as confiscatory tax rates ranging up to 90 percent if he got all his money in one year. By taking what he was owed over several years, he not only insured his future but paid taxes on it each year at a much lower rate. The only trouble was that the book earned him well over a million dollars in a short time. He suddenly realized that even at the interest rates prevalent at the time—around 4 percent—Doubleday would earn more than $25,000 a year from his money by doing nothing more than putting it in a bank. Thus he could contemplate their being able to pay him forty years' worth of $25,000 payments and fulfill their obligation to him but never have to give him the million at all. He decided that he wanted his money, but before breaking his contract or altering it, he sought a ruling from the tax court. The court said that he could indeed insist on getting his money if he wished but that then the whole amount would be ordinary income and taxed as such. It also ruled that if "constructive title" to the money passed to him, then it would stand as his money at that point and also be fully taxable. "Constructive title" would pass to him if Doubleday did any one of the following things: 1. pay interest on the money; 2. set up a separate account with the money that was invested in a business other than publishing, or, 3. used the money in any way other than in the normal course of its regular business. In short, it was either Doubleday's money or it was his and could not be anything in between.

Faced with the choice of ending up with about 10 percent of his money now, about $100,000, which would be four years' worth of $25,000 payments, or settling for his forty years of $25,000 payments, he, of course, chose the forty years. Doubleday thus was handed a million dollars of working capital that it paid no interest on and never had to pay out. It was an unexpected, unplanned, and largely ignored development, but *The Caine Mutiny* ruling became the basis of business practices that soon spread to other authors and other houses. As soon as a house would see a potential best-seller on the horizon, its managers would explain to the author and his agent the advantages of a limiting clause, and everybody would proceed accordingly. It became common practice and remained so for a long time. Whether it is now considered worth doing at today's tax rates, I don't know, but I would imagine it still goes on.

What should be noticed from all this is that it had two profound effects on the publishing scene in the last thirty years or more. It meant that, first, withheld royalties provided the working capital to fuel the enormous expansion that took place in the postwar years for those houses that were able to have big books and authors, and, second, it magnified even more the importance of best-sellers. It turned the big houses into bigger houses, created best-seller mania, and helped the general trend toward driving out the middle-sized firm. It also explains the reasons behind the seemingly ridiculous size of the advances that some big-time publishers have been willing to put up for potential best-sellers. Suppose that a sophisticated moneyman is contemplating the size of an advance and is not making the usual calculation of whether income from the book will be adequate to repay the company its advance. Or suppose that he is making quite another calculation, which is whether the amount of money that does come in will be enough so that the interest generated from it will cover some years of annual payments to the author. If that is the case, then the only figure the moneyman really cares about is the size of the yearly authors' payment, and that is not the kind of thing that gets reported in *Publishers Weekly*. The practice, incidentally, made quite a few authors rich, in effect if not in appearance, and also turned them into virtual stockholders in the companies that owed them money over many years.

The implications of that position, curiously, does not seem to have led a few rich authors or perhaps their lawyers into making the same kind of demands on managements that regular stockholders do, but one would think that anyone who is owed, say, forty years' worth of payments would have by now found a way to make good his interest.

But if that is the effect of withholding royalties in an open, correct and agreed upon manner, what happens if royalties are not paid for what are essentially shady reasons?

The most serious practice is for a publisher to pay his royalties late, or sometimes not at all. Occasionally, he finds a plausible excuse for delay, but often he doesn't bother and simply doesn't pay. Here we must pause and take a look at matters from both sides.

From the moneyman's point of view, if everything is going along well and the firm is profitable, and if he doesn't want to report any greater profits than he actually made, thereby increasing his tax exposure, then there is no reason not to pay his royalties in full and on time. But suppose that cash flow has become strained, and although he has stretched out payments to printers and suppliers, he is still worried about meeting the payroll and getting his books printed. Where can he find cash? Can he go to the bank and borrow against the value of his inventory? He can, but then he is going to pay a fancy interest rate, and the bank is going to want to look over his shoulder a lot. Can he defer some payments that aren't essential to the running of his business on a day-to-day basis so that the scarce cash he does have is used only for the very most necessary accounts? He can indeed, and he can do so with hardly anyone knowing and without having to pay a cent in interest if he simply delays or stops paying his authors royalties. If a loud scream is heard from some valuable author or his agent, then he makes some excuse—"the royalty department has had a lot of illness lately"—and pays up. If he gets a letter from a lawyer threatening a lawsuit, he pays up. If pressed in a way that might suggest the possibility of unfavorable publicity, he pays up.

These small unpleasantnesses may induce him to pay up on, say, some 10 percent of what he owes, but the important fact is that with the other 90 percent he keeps the float going. If he rides out the storm, then when matters ease up and he is once again worrying about his taxes, then he may catch up. In the meantime, no one is looking over his shoulder and hardly anyone even is aware of what he is doing, but he knows he isn't paying any interest.

In one case in which I was involved, a good old-line company—one with a splendid established reputation and run by the kind of old school gentlemen one comes to trust—started to behave badly. One of its very successful authors was owed a large sum in royalties, but the company decided to withhold them as the result of the threat of a lawsuit against the book. There was indeed the appropriate clause in the contract and indeed a lawsuit, but it was clearly a frivolous one, and in defending it, the publisher was being joined by a movie studio with plenty of money. The author was seriously pressed for cash, and the publisher could well have given him a portion of what was owed and kept him happy, but instead the company stood firm on their technical legal ground and gave him nothing. The publisher gave him statements, but they didn't have on them certain quite significant earnings that the author knew had been due. In short, these nice people, the very kind who belonged to all the best clubs in town and sat on the most respected industry boards, started to behave like cheats. It later came out that these good people were in fact in very serious financial trouble and the firm was soon to be bought out by another larger one—but in the meantime, what was the author to do? Could he sue them? How would he pay for it and was it worth it anyway? He discovered with a shock just how little power he really had.

There is one safeguard that an author does have, and it should be in every contract, namely, a clause which allows an author to hire his own accountants to examine the publisher's books. Obviously, an author should invoke this clause only as a last resort or when he is pretty sure that a large sum is involved. It costs money to hire accountants, and since they are seldom familiar with how a publisher's books are kept, it may take them a while to find what they think they need. In addition, of course, such a move always makes an enemy of the publisher, no matter what the accountants find. One change that has taken place in publishing over the past few years that has improved matters considerably for both authors and publishers is the introduction of computers to a publisher's record keeping. In the old days, when everything was done by hand, the amount of paperwork that was required to keep track of what was going on even in a small firm was staggering. The book business always has been plagued by a vast number of small transactions, each of which is as complicated as any big transaction, so computers came as welcome relief to most houses, which saw

quite correctly that this modern-day technology was ideally suited to the problems of publisher's record keeping.
The big houses went over to them first, and now even the
smallest are benefiting from their use. What it has meant
for authors is that royalty information can be provided for
in every invoice as it is first made out, and all the complicated details of royalty calculation can be introduced so
that the figures can be called up at any time. This has
made it harder to cheat and far less worth the trouble, so
anyone who is getting computerized royalty statements
can have some security in knowing that his statement is
generated by the same computer input that also generates
the figures the publisher himself uses in keeping track of
his business. The only thing that the computer won't
report is what is never put into it—so all monies that may
come in from outside sources such as foreign rights, movie
companies, and in fact everything except book sales,
should be asked about with especial care.

Before we leave the subject of royalties, one more seemingly small detail that must be understood—the reserve
for returns.

Because books are sold on a returnable basis, a publisher doesn't really know if a true sale has been made
when he bills and ships a book because it may well come
back later. Most publishers limit the amount of time during which a book may be returned to one year, meaning
that only those sales that are a year old can be regarded as
absolute. But nobody can conduct a business that doesn't
collect on sales for a year, so sales are taken to be real as
they occur and are billed accordingly. If a book is returned, then the bookseller gets credit and may substitute
another book for the first one ordered. For the individual
author, who got credit for a sale when the order was
placed, if his book comes back, his account must have the

appropriate royalty amount deducted instead of added. In order that authors not be asked to pay back cash if returns come in some months after sales appear to have been made, the original contract provides that the publisher may withhold from royalty payments a "reasonable reserve that in its opinion will allow for returns." This is the old standard clause, and it clearly does not limit what a publisher may take to be "reasonable."

When some authors got burned over that one, good agents used to insist that the reserve for returns not exceed 10 percent of the amount owed, and for many years I used that clause. In recent years, however, some publishers have experienced what can only be described as instances of disastrous returns. Some years ago, I heard of one well-known publishing company who in one season had had returns of 45 percent of everything they sent out. This was a consequence of the mad search for a best-seller and an attempt to flood the market as a way of getting one. It is, of course, self-correcting, for such things will break any company in short order, as the costs of manufacturing, billing and shipping all those books must be paid for whether the sales were real or not. But even good publishers were sometimes getting badly stung, so as one way to mitigate their exposure, they began to ask for larger reserves for returns in their contracts. Some companies insisted that the reserve be 25 percent of what was owed, and I heard that others asked for even more. Whatever the figure that is now customary, the point is that any regular amount that may be withheld for a royalty period increases the publisher's permanent float by that amount.

Let us assume that a publisher has managed for the past few years to sign contracts that allow him to keep a 20 percent reserve for returns. An author gets, after all, 80 percent of what he is owed and should get the balance on the next statement, so most of them have gone along with this. What does it mean to a publisher? It means that if all his royalties run upward of 20 percent of his accounts payable, and 20 percent of that may be retained as a permanent revolving float, then 4 percent—3.8 percent in fact—of his debts that are actually never paid, but are an interest-free loan to his firm. This assumes, of course, that he manages his business well and that the actual returns are far less than the 20 percent he has withheld. Inasmuch as returns eat into his float, so do they into his cash position. If his actual returns were what most big firms were accustomed to when I knew about such things, 7 percent or 8 percent would cover a well-managed firm. If he is keeping 20 percent though, then his float is only actually going to be 12 percent of what he keeps, but it is still not a figure to ignore or think to be beneath one's attention.

We have looked at all these complexities for a reason. They begin to illustrate how little of a publisher's true condition may be learned from his balance sheet and the manner in which a good moneyman's mind works. The above calculations will never appear anywhere in an accountant's report and will not, in fact, show in any of the reports the moneyman will see that are generated inside his own house. They are only useful to him as guides to policy and for others as a way to understand his motives.

Books are objects. They are, in fact, very durable objects. Books that were printed hundreds of years ago are still readable and useful. Until the introduction of acid into the paper-making process around the turn of the century, both paper and bindings were of good quality and durable. Now that the destructive effects of acid are being understood, we may be nearing the day when books will again be as physically durable as they once were. Nowadays a publisher may buy paper that is acid free and guaranteed to last a hundred years. Even though the books produced today may be subject to early destruction, they still are good for some dozens of years at least. My copy of *The American Language* by H. L. Mencken was printed in 1921 and is perfectly usable and should stay that way for another fifty or sixty years. Any decently made book is not only durable as an object, it has other attractions. It is handy to get at and to use. It is easily storable and retrievable. It is, in fact, viewed strictly as a technological information retrieval system, cheap, highly efficient, tamper proof and durable. Even if viewed strictly in technical terms, it will be a long time before books are displaced by computers.

There is an additional benefit to books that is so taken for granted that most people do not understand it to be central to the very concept of what a book is—that each is an error-free copy of every other book made from that printing. For practical purposes, each book is identical to every other one that was made on the same press at the same time. There is no chance at all that the single copy you have will contain, say, a misspelling that does not appear in other books of the same title and printing. When you buy a bible or a dictionary or even a murder mystery, you are sure that each copy reads as does every other copy—and it is this strict commonality that makes books the wonderful devices that they are.

What does all this mean to a publisher? It means that he makes books in batches known as printings, and he usually has on hand some copies of his last printing which he keeps as stock to sell to people as they wish to buy more copies. He thus has an inventory of each of the books that he offers for sale, and if his inventory of a given book runs out, he can order another batch so that he may restock his inventory and go on selling that title. He can, of course, decide not to order a new printing, in which case the book is out-of-stock and may be soon declared out-of-print. We will look into that later, but for now we will consider the consequences of his continuing to keep his titles in print and therefore maintaining an inventory at all times.

If royalties are a largely hidden subject, then inventories would stand as their opposite, for they are one of the most visible and much discussed matters in all publishing. Everybody from the author to the buyer seems to care about them, but we will consider them from the point of view of the publisher's moneyman, for the competent management of his inventory is one of his most important tasks.

First, what is an inventory worth? Accountants, tax examiners and the businessman themselves all need to put a figure on an inventory at some moment in time, usually the firm's fiscal year end. Here is a warehouse full of books. What are they worth? An accountant must use some conventions, and we need not go into them here, except to note that the conventions can vary quite a lot. Inventory can be carried at cost and not written down at all until it is sold, or it can be carried as depreciating at some arbitrarily arrived at rate, or it can be handled in various other ways. In addition, it may carry some assigned value as representing its nonphysical value, such as inventory which is kept strictly in order for a book to formally remain in print and thus maintain the validity of a contract. We need not wrestle with the technical complexities here, but note that, in general, the rules of the tax system in recent years have made it more costly for publishers to keep slow-moving inventory. Publishers objected to the idea of having books treated as being no different from spare parts on the shelf of a hardware store, but they adjusted in due course. Clearly a good moneyman and his tax advisors will know the technical details of accounting and adjust their system to reduce their tax liabilities as much as possible. What is interesting to outsiders, though, is not technical values, but true values.

When a publisher receives a shipment of books from his printer and puts them in his warehouse, he fully hopes and expects to sell all of them. If it is a first printing, he will already have taken orders for the books, and a good portion of them may be billed and shipped out within days of physical receipt. Then they will continue to go out as orders come in until that stock is gone and it is time to order more. Or, perhaps better, it is time to consider whether to order more. That question, of course, will have occurred to the moneyman long before the stock has actually run out, and he will usually have made the decision in enough time so that the new stock comes in before the old runs out. A good seller will have many printings. A book that proves to be a dud will have only its first printing. In that case, the unwanted books will simply sit in the warehouse until the publisher gets rid of them by "remaindering" them or having them pulped. Clearly, then, the value of a book can vary from full value to zero, depending upon its saleability, and saleability means not just whether it will be bought but how fast it will be bought. It is when we begin to think this way that we will understand the moneyman and leave the accountants to their fictions.

To begin to evaluate an inventory, then, what you need to know is not only what is on hand, but how well it is selling, and thus you need to know the characteristic selling curve of the type of books at hand as well as how many are in stock. By looking at rate of sale against existing stock, you can get an idea of how long any given stock will last. You may have a few weeks' supply on hand or a few years' supply. Are the books that you are going to sell three years from now worth the same as books that you are pretty sure of selling next month? Most people don't think so, but just how they evaluate that will make a subtle difference to the true meaning of the numbers that appear on their balance sheet.

In the trade book business, there are essentially three different kinds of books and three characteristic sales patterns. A popular novel will have a big sale all at once, over perhaps no more than six weeks, and then suddenly stop entirely. A very popular book such as a best-seller will also have a very brisk sale for quite a while, but once it falls off the best-seller list, its sale drops so quickly as to amaze even the oldest hands. A nonfiction book will have its initial sale over a longer period, and once the first excitement dies down, will settle into a low but steady sale that may last for several years. A staple book is just that, a steady seller that goes along roughly at the same level from year to year. Some nonfiction books pass into being staple books after their initial sale, but that is relatively rare. What this all means for inventory value and management is that the moneyman must know what he may expect of a given book and deal with its inventory accordingly.

The worst disaster that can befall a publisher, and one that has happened to everyone I have ever heard of, is to have a hot seller on which he has just ordered a big new printing suddenly go dead. Once ordered and in work, the printing will arrive whether it is saleable or not. I once had a big new printing of a book I thought was going to sell out very quickly instead suddenly become a total loss. If I had let the first printing sell out, which it did, I would have made a profit and people would be clamoring for copies and exchanging them at a premium. Since I had a second edition come in just as the publicity furor over the book blew over and people lost interest, I found myself getting returns from booksellers just as I was having to pay for the unneeded edition, taking whatever profit there would have been on the first edition and flushing it down the drain.

Some years ago, we had a public and instructive demonstration of good and bad inventory management. Two publishers both had the second book by a writer who had made a terrific splash on the first, each a huge best-seller. In one case, there was a macho male who was with a conservative old-line publisher. In the other, there was a feminine sexpot, a writer of popular costume romances, who had been lured away from her first publisher by an upstart with a lot of money and little experience, but who counted on this new book to be a best-seller, thus both establishing the new house and justifying to its backers the editor's probity in getting a big name author, even if for a fancy price. In each case, the editors of the respective houses knew that what they had was a lousy book. What happened? The conservative publisher printed 50,000 copies of the macho author's new effort, and on the strength of his fame, managed to sell around 42,000 over the first three months after publication. The sale stopped dead then, and the 8,000 copies left over trickled out over the following four years, during which time the conservative publisher added the profits from this enterprise to his already healthy balance sheet. The upstart, however, printed 100,000 copies of its book and spent a lot of money in advertising and promotion while insisting that the trade take a big advance. Once again, on the strength of the author's fame, they sold 42,000 copies before the sale fell dead. They had managed to push out almost 50,000 in advance, so they got back about 8,000 copies and still had

50,000 sitting in the warehouse. It was, of course, a financial disaster, and instrumental in driving the firm from the trade book business. Note that in each case the total sale was the same.

The point for the moneyman to remember is that there are really two quite different types of demand for books. The first is firm and specific. If I decide that I want to read *Adrift*, then I will obtain it somehow, whether by buying it in a bookstore or asking a friend to lend it to me, or putting my name on a list at the local library. I want that book and no other. The second kind of demand is amorphous. If I go into a bookstore and I am looking for a present to take an old sea captain who is lying in a hospital, then I may buy *Adrift* because a seaman may like such a story, or I may just as well take the fellow the new Ludlum or Ken Follett. Anybody who has worked in a bookstore knows that there are essentially two kinds of buyers, those who want something specific and know what it is before they come in, and those who don't really know what they want and who are open to suggestion. The moneyman must be aware that almost all novels are books of weak demand and almost all nonfiction generates a much more specific demand. A sales manager never wants to be in the position of saying that he can't supply a book, so he urges the publisher to always have plenty on hand, but a moneyman must be wary of such enthusiasm, for it leads to warehouses full of books for which the demand suddenly stopped.

A good moneyman knows that if he has a hot novel going and he runs out of books, he must be very careful because if it takes very long for the new printing to come in, the demand will have evaporated. A wait of six weeks, for example, on a novel is just too long. People will have gone on to other things by then. Thus he must order before the stock runs out or risk having the sale stop entirely. This means that managing the sale of a popular novel is tricky and is best done by experienced hands. It also means that a good nonfiction book can stand being out of stock for a while because the demand is pretty specific and not so time-dependent, and that means that prudent inventory management is both easier and safer.

The two extremes of inventory management can best be illustrated by examples. I remember once visiting a good old-line publisher in London to see if we could do any business there. I looked at their list and realized that, although they were publishing a couple of dozen books a year, the firm was slowly dying, and that the people running it had changed nothing since Victorian days. They were very proud of the fact that they had over 4,000 titles in print and their backlist was one of the wonders of British publishing. I had a vision of a huge warehouse out on the edge of the industrial slums of London where every morning one old man in a shiny waistcoat would take a handwritten list of books and clip it on a board and, with a boy pushing a handcart, pick out one by one from the dusty stacks a copy here and then a copy there until the day's orders were filled. Then the two of them would wrap the books one by one in stiff brown paper, fasten them around with string, make out the labels by hand, and leave them at the post at the end of the day. In this way, they would sell from a few to some dozens of each title that was moving every year. Perhaps half the inventory would not sell a single copy in a year, but since so many books were represented by only a few copies, they kept them anyway. I guessed that by the time the boy with the handcart became the man in the waistcoat and the old man with the waistcoat retired, the whole inventory would turn over perhaps once.

Then there was the hustling remainder dealer I visited in his cavernous floors at the old Brooklyn Navy Yard, where he rented space for a song. He had around him a whole crew of sinewy youths, none of whom could read English, and so didn't waste any time reading books. They ran around reading numbers and throwing books in hampers which all came to a central packaging operation that shipped out hundreds of cartons every hour. The dealer wouldn't tell me, of course, but I got the impression that he felt that if his whole inventory didn't turn over at least six times a year, he wasn't doing well at all.

What it comes down to is that a publisher's inventory can only be evaluated by an experienced sales manager who has at hand a record of the recent sales history of every title before him. He can put a reasonable guess on the future of every book in stock, and from that a moneyman can get a firm idea not only of what is on hand but of what its future may be. Some books will be reprinted over and over again, while others will be let go as soon as current stock is gone. Some new books will come into the inventory from new publication, and some simply will have to be gotten rid of, but if the moneyman has some idea of his turnover as against industry average turnover, he will also have a good idea of the true value of what he has.

The true value of inventory is a clear case of the pitfalls of the accountant's assumption—that values can be averaged over a lot of books. The accountant will assume that some books will sell out at full price within a few months, some will sell out over a longer period of time, and some will have to be remaindered. He sets up mathematical models for each happenstance and then puts them together by assuming that a certain percentage of the stock falls in each category. Thus by a suitable manipulation of

216

the numbers in his computer, he can arrive at what he thinks and what he will convince many others is a reasonable estimate of the value of the whole. This kind of exercise goes on every day, and hundreds of perfectly rational people think they are dealing with reality, but they are wrong. I have seen a whole warehouse full of books in which there wasn't a single saleable book, and the inventory was worth, in truth, hardly more than the value of the books as pulp, less the cost of shipping them out. I have also seen a warehouse full of fine books, every one of which was worth its full value and some were already worth a premium above their official price. These are not hypothetical examples, by the way, and while I will slide by the name of the paperback house with the warehouse full of junk, I will note that the good books were all published by Barre Publishers, a firm I bought on behalf of Nat Wartels.

A moneyman, looking at his numbers and the performance of the books his company publishes, should have an idea of what sort of publishing is going on and whether his strategies are reasonable. There are two kinds of trade publishers, front list houses and backlist houses. All academic and scholarly publishing may be said to be strictly backlist publishing, although they are as subject to the vagaries of fashion as anyone else. Front list publishers will have a lot of fiction, most of it aimed at the best-seller list, and backlist houses will have much more nonfiction, a much lower profile, and most probably fewer outright failures. Fiction houses have higher risks but on occasion higher rewards. The really huge jackpots almost never accrue to nonfiction, and as we have seen in our consideration of withheld royalties, the big jackpots can and have transformed the entire nature of a house, so there are always those who seek them. How they do so runs from the shotgun approach to the pinpoint approach, so we will look at each policy separately.

The public demand for fewer and better books, at least from the publishers themselves, has been heard ever since *Publishers Weekly* started keeping track of the business. Some actually try publishing very few books but publish them so well and give them so much support that each has a true chance at a very big sale. They never take a book that they expect to have a so-so reception, much less one that risks outright failure. It is a luxury not available to many, but I learned from the editor of a mass market paperback house not long ago how he was able to be pretty sure of success before he took a book. He handled the hardcover publications of his house, and most of the books he dealt with were ones that had been signed up for their mass market potential. Thus he was able to pick only those from that pool that he thought would do well in hardcover. In short, he was publishing backward from the traditional pattern. Instead of a mass market reprinter seeing how well a book did in hardcover before making a bid on its reprint rights, he was able to see what reprint editors thought of a book as a candidate for mass appeal before thinking of it as a candidate for the trade. Of course, his batting average was very high, and, of course, he was willing to be candid about the fact that he didn't bother to put into hardcover some books that well could have been offered that way and indeed might have been by another publisher. He didn't need to bother with marginal books and was glad of it.

Others are not so lucky, but they don't have to go the whole distance from that kind of selectivity all the way to the other extreme, which I call shotgun publishing. The purest example of that which I ever had anything to do with was the first novel list that Doubleday put out the year I was the firm's advertising manager. In that one year, Doubleday published 104 first novels. Of these, two were great best-sellers and made huge sums of money. Another half dozen definitely made money, but the amount was difficult to determine because it depended on what the book was charged with as a cost. All the others had lost money. Thus Doubleday shot 104 pellets at a target and over 90 percent had missed it entirely. Why would anyone do this? The answer lies in examining what is meant by "losing money."

With a first novel, the publisher will have to use his own staff for manuscript preparation and contract for outside typography, printing and binding. Clearly if he does not recover the outright costs he has incurred to get the book in print, then he has lost money absolutely. But if he sells some of the book, but not enough to cover costs plus what he charges for his own overhead, he may think he has lost money even if it hasn't gone out in cash. But clearly, even if only a few copies were sold, *some* money will have gone toward his overhead. Whether or not the book has paid its costs, then, will depend upon how much he assigns to his own overhead. We will come back to this question shortly, but for the moment we should note that when a publisher says he has not made money on a book, what he means is that there is no clear profit, not that no money came in at all. It also meant in this case that most of those first printings sold on average about half of what was printed. Using dollars as they were valued at the time, let us say that the ninety books that "lost money" were calculated to have "lost" around $3,000 each, then the total "loss" would have been $300,000. But the clear profit on the two winners was around $300,000 *each,* so clear and real profits were twice book losses. The whole enterprise of publishing all those books then showed a handsome profit.

Were there any other values served by going to all that trouble? Yes, there were, but most of them didn't show up on the balance sheet. Without them however, the firm would not have been building the values that would show up in balance sheets some years down the line. All that effort did many things for the publisher, but perhaps most importantly it gave exposure to a lot of new writers and got many careers started. Without all those first books, there wouldn't be second books, and without some first exposure, some important writers would not become established. It is notable that many writers who later went on to fame and fortune did first books that were quite weak, but some editor saw promise and was right. All those commercially unsuccessful books, then, are in fact the publishers' market research. The lesson of *One Book/ Five Ways* which we have already noted, is plain enough, and that is that the same manuscript can make any number of different final books—and it is only in its final published form that any assessment of a book's attractiveness can be made. A bad jacket can kill a book. A terrific review and an especially attractive quote from a famous person who has read the book in galleys can, on the other hand, launch a whole new career. A book that can't even get some good reviews is simply going to disappear. The point is that the only way you can possibly know how a book will be received is to try it and see. Fashion, timing, luck—and who knows what else—all come into play. It used to be that publishing houses were thought to be hopelessly backward because they never did any market research, but that was only because the outsiders who made such statements didn't understand that publishers were doing market research every time they published a book.

But if you did publish a book and then it seemed to sell very well, at what point could you say to yourself that it was making money? This seemingly straightforward question turned out to present more difficulties than I could have imagined, and to this day I cannot give it a clear and unqualified answer. It is, however, a central question and so it must be dealt with both theoretically and as a practical day-to-day matter.

Here is how it started for me. I was editing Western novels at Doubleday, and Walter Bradbury, my boss, asked me to help him in getting out a big picture book on Charles M. Russell, a western artist known as the cowboy painter. The doctrine at the time was that books full of color pictures could not be published by Doubleday because the production costs were too high, but this one was an exception, because it would use existing color plates that had been made for a magazine and that we did not have to remake to use, thus saving us large amounts of money. I did work on the book and when it was published, it was very successful indeed, so I then wanted to see if we could do more books of a similar nature. I got involved with one on Frederick Remington, and it was in doing the estimates for this that my education proceeded.

The book business is dominated by percentages, and an editor has to deal with them whenever he plans a new book. Each book will have a plant account and a per copy paper, printing and binding figure. The plant account is the total of all the costs that are expended in order to produce the first copy of the book. They are all one-time expenses and include editorial costs (if they are outside charges), design charges (again, if they are hired from the outside), typesetting, proofing, and all photography, general prep and platemaking needed before the first copy can come from the press. All these costs are added up, become the plant account, and are usually expected to be paid out of the sale of the first edition. Thus the per copy plant account will depend on the size of the first edition, so that a 5,000 copy first edition which has, say, a $2.00 plant account will have only a $1.00 plant account if the edition is 10,000. The plant account number is added to the regular paper and printing cost, which does not vary from one copy to another, and the total is then taken to be the cost of the book per copy over the first edition.

The total cost per copy is then used as a fixed percentage of the retail price of the book. This percentage varies from house to house, and it has varied over the years, becoming steadily lower in the last thirty years, but for our purposes we will say that the manufacturing cost of a book is twenty percent of the retail price. A $20.00 book then will have actually cost the publisher $4.00 in manufacturing costs, and an editor contemplating a new book will know what the book has to be sold for if he first figures out what it will cost. All he has to do is multiply by five.

It should perhaps be noted that, for many publishers, the plant account means something different from what I describe here. It often means the whole manufacturing cost of the first edition. Also, clearly, the per copy cost of paper, printing and binding is not absolutely fixed and independent of the quantity printed either, for paper costs less per unit as you order larger quantities. Nonetheless, to me it seems most instructive to think of one-time charges as the plant account and the paper, printing and binding (PPB) as a fixed cost per copy.

222

In thinking about a proposed new art book, then, two things are crucial—the outright plant account costs and the size of the first edition. If your book is going to have eighty full-color plates, each costing $450.00, and then is going to have a first run of 5,000, you are then spending $7.20 per copy for plates alone, so with all the other charges you are looking at a book that will retail for $50.00. But will people pay fifty dollars for your book? Probably not. So what can you do? Suppose that you decide on half as many plates and twice as many books in the first printing. In that case the plates are only going to run $1.80 a book, and together with other costs the manufacturing price per copy will be about half your original estimate, or about $5.00 a copy, so now you have a book that will sell at $25.00 retail. That clearly is going to be easier to sell— remembering only that 10,000 is twice as many as 5,000, and maybe the market for this book at any price is around 6,000-7,000.

That is, you think that there are enough serious fans who will buy a book at more or less any price, and enough libraries that will also have to have this book at more or less whatever price it is, so that you could have a sale of perhaps 4,000 at no matter what price, while the extras over 4,000 will come from those who would like the book but will only buy it at a price that seems both reasonable and affordable. Thus you can have a very expensive book for the fans and do 5,000 at $50.00, or you can do a more popular book of 10,000 at $25.00. You can, in fact, juggle the numbers and get something in between as well. It is at this point that you solicit opinions from people who have been around a while and also from a sales manager. In my case, I went further and talked to the general money manager.

He took me in hand and explained the basic percentages. Using a $10.00 book for ease of figuring, the first thing to realize is that because of the discount schedule, it can be assumed that over the average of all books sold, fifty-four percent of the retail price of a book comes in to the publishing company, or in our case, $5.40. This is then allocated as follows: 40 percent is assigned to general office overhead—that is, 40 percent of what comes in or $2.16 in our example—then $2.00 is allowed for manufacturing, and $1.00 or 10 percent of retail is allowed for royalty, and after all these numbers are added up you will find that twenty-four cents turns out to be profit. This assumes that the whole first edition is sold.

I asked why the number for overhead was so high. Didn't you start to make money as soon as the manufacturing was paid off? In our example, $20,000 would have been spent in direct manufacturing, so doing a few simple sums would suggest that 3,700 copies sold would bring back the $20,000 and then everything that came in after that could be regarded as contributing to overhead. No, I was told, you couldn't figure it that way. For one thing, every sale carried a royalty payment that was a liability, so even using my assumptions, it couldn't be $5.40 that was earned back, but $4.40. So even doing it my way, it would take about 4,500 books to earn back the manufacturing cost. Well, even so, it seemed that if all books could be thought of as being in the black when half the first edition was sold, then things weren't so bad. No, I was told, the overhead keeps having to be paid anyway, so just earning back manufacturing doesn't really do anything for you. Well, yes, but why was overhead such a big slice of what came in?

Here I ran into the gentle condescension that comptrollers reserve for young editors. Look around you, he said. Here we all are sitting in Madison Avenue offices, among the most expensive in the country. You get a salary. Your secretary gets a salary. I get a salary. You use the phone and the lights, and you take your authors to lunch in good French restaurants. You travel. You ask us to promote and advertise your books. You expect us to have salesmen, and a warehouse, and people to do packing and shipping and then send bills out and collect the money. All this and more are required in order to be in the business, and this is called overhead, and it has to be paid whether or not what you do brings in money.

I knew that there was no use arguing about all that, but it still rankled that, because we were obliged to assign a fixed 40 percent to overhead, it made expensive books too hard to do. Why was it that other firms could publish picture books and sell them for a reasonable price and we could not? Wasn't it because we were tied to an arbitrary figure? I tried a new tack. Why, I asked, couldn't you add up the firm's entire overhead for a whole year, and then divide it into the average number of books published in a year, and thus come up with a dollar figure that should be earned back from each book in order to cover overhead? By doing that, you would get a dollar number for each book just as you had a dollar number for manufacturing. Wasn't the problem caused by the fact that an expensive book was asked to pay a huge amount to overhead by virtue of the percentage system? A $20.00 book was paying four times the amount that a $5.00 book did. (This was in the early fifties and a good solid book sold for $5.00). Couldn't they think in terms of dollars instead of percentages? I was told that they could not.

I tried yet another tack. Why, then, was the overhead so high? Did it include, for example, the trade department's share of running the company plane? Yes, the comptroller said, overhead covered all the expenses of the firm as a whole. But I pointed out that the trade department didn't need a company plane, never used the company plane, and would, if asked about it, get rid of it immediately. Why should we have to pay a share of something that was of no use to us? The comptroller grew exasperated. The company plane and everything else were simply part of general overhead and neither he nor I could do anything about it—so what else was it that I wanted to know? I was still frustrated, so I tried going back a little. I said, well, suppose that I do an estimate for an art book that is going to sell for several times the price of a regular book. Acknowledging that it would bring in many more overhead dollars than a regular book even if it sold no more copies than any other book, could I then use a lower overhead figure just for that book in compensation? Could we then publish art books, books of quality and price that would be equal to what others were doing? No, I was told firmly. If we let you use anything but the regular figure, then we will have to let others do it as well or else there would be a terrific outcry.

At this point I stopped arguing, for what I had come up against was not something rational but something political. If it was essentially political that things were set up as they were, then I as a very young editor could hardly hope to assault that citadel.

In sum, what I was stuck with was this:

Retail price	100%
Amount received by publisher	54%, divided as follows:
Overhead	21.6%
Manufacturing ...	20%
Royalty	10%
Profit	2.4%

Contemplating these figures and using them on a daily basis in making estimates, a number of effects become evident in trying to fit them into any plan for making a workable book package. The first thing that becomes obvious is that a twenty cent saving in the manufacturing cost translates into a dollar saving at retail. Let us, for example, go back to our original estimates for an art book when we wanted to have eighty color plates. Then we thought that the cost of a color plate was $450.00. Suppose that I find a very good platemaker who only charges $150.00 for one set of four color plates. Then instead of having to pay $36,000 for the plates, the cost would be $12,000. Thus, the expensive plates would require $17.50 of retail money for the plates alone, while the cheaper plates would require only $6.00. In fact, if the color plates cost that much, I could probably figure out everything else in such a way as to bring out a nice book with eighty plates in color for a retail of $20.00. Now I would have an attractive and competitive book. This illustrates the dramatic effect of the seemingly small differences in manufacturing costs. It seems that almost all publishers work on the same percentages, or at least on a system of percentages, so it explains their constant drive to trim manufacturing costs. This has led on occasion to some very bad publishing decisions. A sales department, for example, will tell an editor that a given book, to sell, ought to be no more than a certain very reasonable price. Sales people always want a lot of book for not much of a retail price because they figure that then more will be sold. The editor then trims the specifications to make the low retail price possible, but in doing so causes the book to look so cheap that no one wants it at any price. This has happened more often than anyone will tell you about, and is usually the error of a young editor who does not know how to stand up to comments from those who are older and supposedly wiser than he.

When I first started estimating art books, I knew nothing at all about the production costs of things like color plates. I had worked before with type and linecuts and halftones, but color was another world. I found out that production people are not trained and cannot be expected to be helpful with estimates. That is, they will never spontaneously show you that by doing things differently you could save money. They will take what you give them and tell you what it will cost using the suppliers with whom they are accustomed to dealing.

Here, in passing, it should be noted that the phrase "the suppliers that they are accustomed to using" hides an enormous and very complicated subject that we cannot go into at length here. Suffice it to note that publishers are creatures of habit and a production department actually has little incentive to set up new relationships. Since the cost of production is one of the largest outlays that a publishing house makes, the credit relationships that exist between it and its suppliers are crucial to the management of its cash flow, and a good ongoing working relationship between a publisher and a printer is of great advantage to both parties. The effect of this is that most production departments operate within a quite narrow range of suppliers and a familiar style of books.

What all this meant was that if I wanted to publish art books there would be no substitute for learning enough about the production of color plates to virtually do for the production department what it was then not doing for itself or for me. I didn't get that education then, but I had to later.

In the meantime, it was obvious that if the cost of manufacturing was of the greatest importance to being able to publish art books, then the only other "cost" that could be manipulated was, of course, royalty. If twenty cents could be saved in royalty, the publisher would save the same dollar in retail price as would manufacturing cost. I asked around and found that royalty did seem indeed to be something that could be manipulated. I had been amazed at what the firm of Harry N. Abrams was putting on the market, and couldn't understand how he did it. The answer seemed to be that, among other things, he managed to pay very low royalty rates on what he did. It was all nothing but rumor and hearsay, of course, but the story that I got ran something like this.

Harry would decide that he could sell a big lavish art book about some rising young abstract expressionist and would tell the artist that he wanted to do such a book. He would point out that a book would have a huge positive effect on the value of the artist's work. His gallery would be able to raise his prices by very large sums, his name would be established in a way that no other public event could match, and all the pictures that were illustrated in the book not only would be authenticated by their inclusion, but also would command premium prices. All in all, an artist could and should regard a book about him as the most effective promotion piece imaginable, and there were thus compelling reasons for him to make it possible for Abrams to put out to the public the most extravagant art book possible but one still affordable by his admirers. All the foregoing, by the way, was perfectly true.

In any case, this meant that the subject of the book and the author of whatever text there was agreed to accept very low royalties indeed, as collecting royalties was almost beside the point. This also meant that Abrams was able to put very much more into production costs than anyone who was paying regular royalties or anything near them. There were also rumors about other things, but I never found out if they were true. Harry was widely admired as being an operator, and it was said that whenever he published a book about an artist, he managed to get the artist to give him a painting. It was also said that when he had accumulated enough paintings, he used to pledge his art collection to the bank every fall to raise the money needed to produce that season's books. It was an outrageous story and nothing but hearsay, and I didn't know whether to believe it, but it sure didn't sound like what I had learned about how Doubleday operated.

When I started my own company and wanted to do picture books, I realized that one which is all text is a very simple affair and easy to estimate and make. It can be regarded as the author's book. However, a picture book, since how it looks depends so much on the dozens of small decisions a publisher and his designer make in organizing it, can be regarded as a publisher's book. It is much more costly and much more subject to becoming unattractive through a publisher's mistakes, so I myself saw that to be able to present the books as I wanted, I would have to find some give somewhere. I often did ask for seven and a half percent royalty on the first edition, and usually was able to persuade an author that it was a reasonable figure. The royalty rate would then go to a normal figure for the second and any subsequent editions.

Here we must pause and consider two very important matters. The first is the profit margin on second editions, and the second is the attractiveness of the books in the first place.

If the cost of each book of the first edition consists of both the plant account and the individual PPB (paper, printing and binding) amount, then the cost of each copy of the next edition consists only of PPB. The plant account may well have been as much as half the cost of each book of the first edition, so clearly if the second edition costs half as much per book as the first, the difference all goes straight to profit. It is for this reason that royalty rates are higher on later editions, and it is for this reason that backlist books are profitable and sustain the health of most publishers.

When I started my own company, I was told that most houses tried to run the company off the backlist and figure to make its profits there, and publishing new books as a break-even business was done only to find and add titles to the backlist. This didn't help me much as I had no backlist, but it was an interesting goal to contemplate.

The second matter was the attractiveness of the books themselves. All publishers either have designers who are on their staff or else use free-lance designers for each book, paying them a fee per book. All manuscripts have to be given precise specifications for the typographer—typeface, size of type, leading, indentations, heads, folios, and all the rest, each element being covered by some instruction, for only then will the typographer know what to do. This has to be done no matter how the final book looks, and it costs as much whether it is done well or badly. Here was one point where I wanted my company to differ from all others—I wanted all the books to look good. It was obvious that a good design costs no more than a bad one, it is merely a matter of taste and style. There are some typefaces that are hard to read and others that are clear, crisp and legible—and one costs no more to use than another. There are clean designs and messy and muddy designs. For exactly the same amount of money you can produce a book that appeals to the eye or one that looks shoddy. I had often enough seen people in a bookstore pick up a book, flip through it quickly and perhaps turn it over to read the back of the jacket, and then either keep it or put it back. What made people decide so quickly to keep a book? It seemed clear to me that how it looked by itself as an object was of more than trifling importance. Most publishers seemed to care very little about such matters, seeming to believe that a book was wanted for its words rather than its looks, but I suspected that just because it was an effect that could never be measured, the physical attractiveness of a book was given far less thought and care than it should. Accordingly, I tried to pay attention to design and I have always felt that it helped greatly to establish the reputation of the firm and, at least in one case, made all the difference between success and failure.

When I was a science editor at Doubleday, I had written Martin Gardner, whose mathematical recreational column ran every month in *Scientific American*, and asked him to lunch. I shall never forget it, for I somehow sensed that it was to be the start of a long association, as it indeed proved to be. He told me that when enough of his columns had been run to make a book, they were collected and that Simon & Schuster published the collection. Every time they did so, they sold about 35,000 copies of the book. This was a very impressive number in 1955—books appeared in the best-seller list that sold no more. He said that he did, however, have some other ideas for books, and that he was not accepting a nice lunch under false pretenses because he actually thought that some of the ideas might interest me. As lunch progressed, he went through each, and one by one I told him that I didn't think it was something for me.

Finally, over coffee, he said that I seemed to be a nice young man, and since that was so, he thought he would mention an idea that he had been working on for the last fifteen years. He said that he had brought it up to every publisher he had met and that every time he had explained it, he was laughed at. In all those years no one had ever taken him seriously, but if I would promise not to laugh at him, he would tell me his idea. I agreed, and he told me that he wanted to do an annotated edition of *Alice in Wonderland,* and of course, I laughed. I actually did. He was duly chagrined, but said that it was really no more than he expected. I said, though, that the reason I laughed was that he had told the one person he knew who would instantly take to the idea. He was then surprised, but I told him that I thought it was a wonderful idea and to tell me more about it. I quickly became convinced that it was a brilliant idea, and I took it back to my colleagues at Doubleday. They laughed at me. Several years later, when I had joined The Dial Press, I persuaded George Joel to sign up Martin for an annotated edition of *Alice,* even though he was very reluctant. When I decided to leave Dial and start my own company, I asked George if I could take over the contract and relieve him of the burden of it, and upon my paying him the thousand dollars he had already laid out in advance for it, I personally acquired the *Alice* contract, and it was the first contract that I brought to the new company.

When it came time to actually prepare to publish the manuscript, I found myself in an awkward position, for I didn't know how we would go about publishing the book. We had to have the complete original text of *Alice* and, of course, all the John Tenniel illustrations in their proper place, for there were quite a few notes about them along with everything else. But how were we going to handle all the notes?

Sydney Butchkes had agreed to do my company colophon and letterhead, and all the rest of the graphics I used. Diana Klemin, who I thought was the best designer at Doubleday, had put me on to Sydney, and I was so pleased with what he had done so far that I persuaded him to do *The Annotated Alice* as well. We had talked about our problem for a long time and had not found a solution. The trouble was that everybody hated footnotes. In a scholarly book, they were customarily on the bottom of the page to which they referred. This made for a page where the eye had to go up and down from the citation to the note and then back again, and do it all again if there was more than one note. It was awkward and annoying and made for a terrible-looking page from the typographical standpoint. There might be a page with no notes, the next one with one or two, and then one where the notes would occupy half the page. I hated the idea of doing things that way.

The situation is neatly summed up in one of Charles Schulz's "Peanuts" cartoons.

Reprinted by permission of UFS, Inc.

But what other way was there? I had tried to read an annotated edition of *Moby-Dick* not long before, and in that case all the notes had been collected at the back of the book. This meant that as I was reading along, I would notice a number. I would then have to stop, go to the back of the book, locate the chapter, and then the number of the note for that chapter. To do it at all required two place marks and a constant flipping back and forth from front to back, and the arrangement seemed so awkward and irritating that I wished at all costs to avoid it.

For me the trouble was that I had announced the book, I had a manuscript, and it was time to set it. Sydney came over to the office and we got into a taxi to go and discuss the book with my production man. It was a sweltering summer day, and as the cab was stuck in traffic on a side street in the sixties, we talked about what we might do. Sydney pulled out a sheet of paper and a pencil and said, well, if we had a pretty big page and ran the text of *Alice* down the inside of each page and then had a huge outside margin, we could put all the notes alongside of what they referred to in a smaller type and thus have them where they belonged. He drew a rough sketch on the paper, holding it on his knees as the sweat dripped off his face. I knew it was right from the minute he explained it. Later, we would refine it a little and think about it more deeply, but, then and now, it was a brilliant solution to a very special and difficult problem. It was such a success, of course, that all the books that came later on in what became a series used the basic design idea that Sydney showed me in the back of the cab. It depends for its success upon the circumstance that in our culture all reading is learned as a scan from left to right on a horizontal line. This is so "natural" to all western people that to ask them to shift their eye focus up and down is to make them feel uncomfortable. It also meant that we would have a succession of regular and good-looking pages, whether or not there were notes, because the text of *Alice* alone looked good just by itself. If there were too many notes for a margin to hold, we would skip the text itself and just print notes until text and notes caught up with each other.

In addition to a wonderful design, there were two other decisions that I made at the time which were unusual and which I was warned against, but which worked out very well. I insisted that we print the book on laid paper, an extra expense that I was assured was not worth it. A laid paper has a series of parallel lines embossed in it that gives it a rough texture, and also makes it seem antique and rich. It did cost more, and even was some trouble to get, but I felt I had to have it. I also decided to ask a round $10.00 for the book instead of the $8.00 or $8.50 that a strict cost accounting would have allowed. I was told I was pricing myself out of the market. This was 1960, after all, when that kind of money was more than the price of a theatre ticket or a decent lunch. I knew, though, that either you wanted this book a lot or you couldn't care less, so those that would think it as wonderful as I did would come up with the money. The book is, of course, still in print and still selling, although the reprint doesn't have laid paper.

If all of this has seemed like a mere digression from the point, which is to attempt to answer the question of how do you know when you are making money, it really shouldn't. It is an attempt to show how complicated things get even if you are in charge of everything and make all the decisions yourself. I think that the only real way you can tell about money is with the jelly bean method. All you do is look at the jelly bean jar and ask whether there are more beans in the jar at the end of the year than there were when you started, and if there are, then you made money. If not, you are losing. I suppose that it's known formally as the cash flow method, and it doesn't tell you anything such as the amount of money you have tied up in inventory, but it certainly does have its uses.

The question, then, of how you tell whether or not you are making money is a complicated and sophisticated matter, and can really only be answered in very general and gross terms. You know that you are losing money if a book does not sell enough to make back its manufacturing costs, and you know pretty much for sure that if you are pricing your books right you are in the black when the first edition sells out and you need to print more. You also know that if you have sold the first edition and some rights money comes in, the rights money is pure profit.

Because rights money is so clearly profit, it has led to some practices that I regard as very poor corporate policy, namely, running the list in such a way that for its success it depends upon rights money. Many publishers will laugh at this position, saying that there is no way to do better than breaking even on the actual publication and sale of books, and that profits come only from rights income, and in truth many of them do run their houses on that basis. I maintain, however, that this is a dangerous way to run a company, for it cannot be sustained over any long term. If a company cannot at least break even on the publication and sale of its books, then I do not wish to be one of its stockholders. Profit and loss, after all, depend as usual on the level of company overhead, and overhead, no matter how much a manager may protest to the contrary, is something that can be controlled.

Shortly after I started my company, I got to know a very fine, wry man called Chip Chafetz. He was, like me, a Western American history buff, and was working on a history of gambling in America which I eventually published. He asked me to visit him at his bookstore, which I did. He owned and ran one of those huge old second-hand Manhattan bookstores down on lower Fourth Avenue that still flourished at that time. It was an enormous place, going back what seemed like hundreds of feet and having another couple of floors above. Of course he specialized in Western Americana, and there were the usual dusty row upon row of old books piled and stacked everywhere. He was very proud of his place and said that it afforded him and his partner a comfortable living. He also mentioned that he was a publisher himself. I expressed interest and he got out a stack of three-by-five cards. Look, he said, here are the cards on each book. We've done half a dozen and they've all made money. I showed interest and he explained. On each card was a listing of all the actual costs of making his edition. The books were reprints of famous old Western history books that were long out of print and unavailable except as rare books. They were all in the public domain, so, of course, there was no royalty to pay. He showed his expenses and his income. In every case, sure enough, there was more income than outgo. See, he said, they are all in the black.

Later on, I gave all that some thought. He considered himself to be in the black on all those books because he didn't charge the books a penny of overhead. His bookstore was, in effect, his backlist. That made money and provided him with a living and also provided his publications with some very necessary things like warehouse space, order processing, shipping, billing, and record keeping. He was doing all those things for his rare book business, so bringing in a stock of a new title hardly added anything on top of what he already was paying for. Really, in a sense his new books didn't have to pay any overhead if he didn't want them to. To him, being in the black simply meant that he had paid off his manufacturing costs. If I were, say, retired in the country and decided to publish a book by having some copies made and then keeping them in my garage and selling them strictly by mail order, wouldn't I be in more or less the same position? Yes, but neither his position nor my supposed one was of any useful instruction to me, because I was trying to do something entirely different, which was to found a real publishing house, and to do that you had to have a lot of overhead. What it came back to, once again, was—how much overhead?

It is in his relationships with the people he employs that a moneyman's talent and wisdom are most seriously tested. He must know whom to place in what slot and how to keep him happy and productive there. In the businesses that I have seen myself, the number of people who were in the wrong job was astounding. The damage that was done to them and to their organizations by such mistakes cannot be measured, but the unhappy history that always results is often all too plain. The trouble, of course, is that the person who is tapped for a given job almost never says to the man who has offered it that he is not the one for the job. He is offered a bigger job, a raise, a title, and usually told that he is taking on a challenge that will give him a chance to demonstrate his talents. He doesn't himself think that he can't do the job—he usually doesn't know what is involved with it anyway—so he says sure, and thinks it's all wonderful. It is only when he finds that he can't make up his mind about things, can't be sure what is right, feels lost and overwhelmed and realizes that he can't hack it, that the real trouble begins. At that point, few admit that they are not where they should be but try to face it out, and it is then that very bad decisions are taken and costly and long-lasting courses are embarked upon. This is no place to point out specific unhappy stories, for almost anyone in publishing can produce several of his own. It is to point out that if this is so, bad mistakes are all too common. They should not be blamed on the unfortunates who cannot manage a job, but on those who put them there in the first place. But how can anyone tell who is capable of what?

Milton Runyon, executive vice president of Doubleday, seemed to think that most jobs could be handled by anyone who had some moderate intelligence and who was willing to work and learn. He offered the job as head of the Literary Guild and all the rest of the many Doubleday book clubs to a young man who was the editor of a sports magazine and had never been in the book business, had no knowledge of the mail-order business, and had never been in corporate management. He was bright and hard working, to be sure, but he was as surprised by the offer as I had been myself some years before when Mr. Runyon offered me the job of advertising manager of Doubleday. I had told him that I was an editor, a working intellectual, a science specialist, and wanted to be nothing more. I knew little of advertising and didn't like what I had heard. I had never run a staff, had no experience in spending large sums of money, and didn't want the job. He said that I would do fine and told me to be at the new desk at nine o'clock the next morning.

Mr. Runyon was right in both cases, for each of us did do the job he put us in. It is interesting to note, however, that each of us soon went on to other things and never really liked the job he picked for us. Perhaps it is just an illustration of the fact that any fool can do most jobs, but I like to think that it is an illustration that it is better for a moneyman to decide something, no matter how far-fetched, than to dither about and leave an important job unfilled.

In any case, if we assume that the moneyman has placed the right people in the right jobs, there is always the question of how many of each kind he needs. Herbert Bailey suggests in his book that a manager should keep his staff lean, but doesn't go very deeply into the idea. A good moneyman, however, will think about the matter and conclude that he should always have fewer people than are needed to do the work of the firm. It is unfortunate but true that overstaffing is the chronic tendency of all bureaucracies regardless of their stated intent. For a private firm aiming at profits, the tendency is more dangerous than it is for a government department. The only way to manage things, therefore, is for the moneyman to have fewer people than he knows he really needs. The department heads should and will object, and he should in turn be objective and allow the regular if not too frequent use of free-lancers to fill the gap. It is especially true in serious text editing, copy editing and design that the time required for any given job can vary enormously. If a designer is going to have to lay out every single page of a book as if it were a whole new design task, and there are plenty of picture books where this has been the case, then weeks or even months may be needed for the job. In that case a wise manager will ask his department head to find an outsider.

The point is that in a well-run firm, everyone will know that the staffs are too small, and that free-lancers can and should be used to fill the gap, while in a less well-run firm, the management will maintain that there are plenty of people to do the jobs asked and that if they cannot do them, the staff must either be lazy or not good at their jobs. This is a very destructive way to run things, in fact, for if a department head can only ask to hire a free-lancer as a last desperate resort, then he and his people are working under too much tension, and good work cannot really be expected from them. Endless jobs done under pressure may seem adequate to an unsophisticated money man, but the firm will turn out the hack work it is paying for and many books that could have done well do not. Here is the trouble. How do you measure opportunity lost? How can you ever quantify something like what might have happened, indeed, what should and would have happened, if a book had been done well when it was done badly? Clearly, you can't. All you ever know is the general reputation of the firm, and I for one am convinced that houses that consistently turn out dreary books are greeted with notably less enthusiasm by buyers than are the representatives of houses known for well-made and good-looking books.

As this brings us straight to the matter of intangibles, it is time now to consider some of the things that don't show up on a balance sheet at all. We have seen how careful one has to be to be in looking at the figures that do appear on the balance sheet. We are now led to a consideration of those things that no one thinks should be quantified, and most prominent among them is the matter of the firm's reputation. Even accountants know that how long a firm has been in business, how well it has done, how respected it is, and its perceived standing in the publishing community are all important in some sense. It is called Good Will in a balance sheet and assigned an arbitrary small figure, but everyone knows that it is important and that the value of a firm rests in no small degree on its reputation.

How is a name built, and what goes into making it what it is? I contend that the crucial matters are the success of its books, the quality of its books and its business dealings, and the continuity and stability of its operations. Having highly saleable books in a consistent way is perhaps the most important thing. They don't all have to be best-sellers, but if a firm seldom puts out books that are true dogs it will come to seem in a way reliable. Some firms have big hits and then a lot of flops, but the hits don't make up for the misses, and so people carefully scrutinize every offering, while other firms will get attention for whatever they put out, for it is taken to be of a certain quality just because it came from that firm.

Nowadays, a firm's business dealings are not likely to be anything but regular and understood, but in the past some individual owners had highly specific methods, some being quixotic, some very mean and tough, some merely sloppy. I used to be infuriated by George Joel's business methods, and soon found out that everyone else either got used to them or didn't do business with him. He admitted to me that he had grown up in the garment business and said that the margins were so thin there that he had perforce learned to be a chiseler. To me what it meant was that if I asked the comptroller for a check for an author's advance for a thousand dollars, as called for in the contract, what I would get was a check for $900. George would say, well, send it along and see if he'll accept it. If he screams, then we'll give him the other $100. I pointed out to him that constantly doing business that way was in fact wasteful, took much more time, made people hate him, and didn't really add anything to profits. He said that he knew all that, but he couldn't do things any other way—it was bred in him.

He even knew that he was eroding the good name of The Dial Press when he constantly played the trimmer, but it was his conscious feeling that the name of The Dial Press was like an asset, and that every time he used that good name to get by with some small shaving of a deal, he was using up a little bit of that asset. He asked me, "How else can I use up the asset? If I don't use it in some way, what value is it?" I pointed out that he was trying to sell the company, and that it seemed to me that he would want the good name of the company kept as pure as possible. Oh, no, he said, the kind of people who might buy the company wouldn't know about how he operated, and the suppliers and authors certainly wouldn't make life any harder for him, so to a buyer the way he did business would not have hurt the value of the name. He would think it as good as it ever was. I told him that I knew how he did business and he had offered the firm to me, so it wasn't true that a potential buyer would not know what he had been doing to the firm's good name, because I knew myself. No, he said, I didn't count. I had already decided not to buy the firm.

Business methods, then, have improved in recent years and are now less subject to personal direction and style than they used to be. In another direction, however, things have gotten worse rather than better, and this is in the matter of continuity. In recent times the internal stability of a firm seems to have been given almost no thought at all, and the turnover of ownership, management and policy has been regular and large. I maintain that continuity is very important to a firm, that it has been abused and abandoned in recent years, and that until it is reestablished at serious firms, that firm will all continue to suffer from the far too many abrupt changes that have characterized recent years. A writer's working lifetime is long, often fifty or more years. Good books last, the best ones becoming staples that have a life as long or longer than that of their creators. A publishing firm should have a life as long as or longer than the best of its books. To make vast internal changes in a firm is to ask everyone to start all over, as if they were starting a new firm. I think that continuity is the least appreciated and one of the most important parts of a firm's components, and to ignore it is to subject the firm to grave danger.

Take that most important relationship—the one that grows up between an author and his editor. If the two of them get along well and, in so doing, get the best book that the author can make, then that bond should not be broken. It is notorious that in recent years managements have ignored this bond and broken it repeatedly, as if expecting that it can always be reestablished in a half hour's conversation with some new person. This destructive attitude has infuriated any number of authors and I feel sure meant poorer books as a result. Nowadays, as we have already seen, some authors have clauses in their contracts that provide for the event of their editor leaving the company, so that the contract is really with the editor rather than the publisher. It is a comment on the transitory nature of editors' jobs that such a clause should be even thought of, let alone be necessary. Those authors who do not have such a clause can find themselves shunted from one to another ignorant and unsympathetic tyro and only conclude from such treatment that they should be looking for another publisher.

For a firm to lose the authors that it has taken the first risk to establish is not a trivial matter. It is true that authors who have a best-seller are often lured away from their publisher by someone who comes along and offers a fat package, but actually these cases are really the exception. The majority of regular professional authors will stay with their publisher unless something disturbs the steady relationship. I used to publish quite a few books in the field of antiques, for example. Few of the books were ever best-sellers and no one ever expected them to be. They were, however, all good sellers in their original editions and almost all of the books went on to have a long life as a hardcover reprint. There were a few firms who did these kinds of books, and everybody in the field knew everybody else. Some authors were so hardworking that they needed two publishers to handle everything they did. I would therefore hear how my authors were handled by other editors, and sometimes the stories I heard were shocking and would result in a publisher losing a bread-and-butter author. The trouble invariably arose when an experienced and knowledgeable editor was replaced by someone who didn't know the job but pretended that he did. Continuity and professionalism would be replaced with ignorance and arrogance, and as a result a perfectly good publishing house would suffer a wound. These wounds are not evident to a student of the balance sheet, and the substance draining away may not even be noticed by the management of the firm itself, but the authors know. They talk to each other, and in time the firm finds that almost all its books are being written by first-time authors, and then it is time to start looking for the announcement of yet another merger.

I do not think that there can be any question but that the careers of Maxwell Perkins at Scribner's and Ken McCormick at Doubleday were the outstanding successes they were because they both entailed a lifetime of work at the same place, so much so that to many the image of the person and the firm were virtually interchangeable. The much-traveled editor who usually seems to stand for the way things are now simply does not command the loyalty, the respect and the trust that his settled counterpart can expect almost as a matter of course. The close coupling of a person to a firm is something to which I can testify by my own example, for I discovered that in a very real sense, when I retired from Clarkson N. Potter, Inc., I was no longer myself. After I left my firm, I found that I was no longer thought of as "Clarkson N. Potter," for my former editor, Jane West, had taken over running the list, and therefore she became "Clarkson N. Potter" rather than I. This loss, or splitting of identity, was something that I had neither anticipated nor been prepared to understand, but it was very odd to have someone say to me, "You're not Clarkson N. Potter anymore, are you?" Mr. Holt and Mr. Morrow and Mr. Doubleday and Mr. Scribner, and all the rest of them, are no longer with us, and yet during their lifetimes, they must have been not only synonymous with their firms but had taken on the dual identity with hardly a thought. This identity of a person with a firm is powerful and important, and yet its value has been ignored when it has not been thoughtlessly discounted by a host of modern money managers. In my view, when moneymen do this, they are throwing away value that has been earned over years and can only be built up again by careful nurturing.

Stability and continuity may be underappreciated when it comes to the people running the firm, but they are well understood to be of great value in straightforward business matters. A long-established firm will have little difficulty in maintaining proper credit terms with its suppliers, and should be able to raise capital when that is needed as well. Companies with steady and reliable balance sheets in fact have less trouble than ones that have spectacular successes and then a couple of poor years. Simply being there is of the very greatest importance, and that is why George Joel insisted that as sick as The Dial Press was at the time, the fact that it was a going business, that it had a good name, that it had credit relationships that could be used, and that it had a couple of energetic young editors were all considerations that could be and should be translated directly into dollars if the company were to be sold. His view of the firm as a living being impressed me then and has never left me, and I have tended to look at firms that way ever since.

The role of the moneyman, then, is a complicated one, and not easily filled. He should preside over and guide a business that is complicated and full of risk, but that depends for its success on an intimate knowledge of its various intertwining parts and the ability to make them work easily together. He must know conventional methods of business and how to apply them as they are appropriate, but he must also know when to bend them to special needs. Most of all he needs good judgment and a deep understanding of the people around him. Only when he can combine them into a dynamic and productive whole will he know that he is doing his best.

Bibliography

This list of books is meant for browsing. It is set up in alphabetic order by title and each book is briefly explained so that a student may decide whether any given book seems worth looking into. A trip through it is encouraged both for serious students and for the more casual wanderer. For the most part, these books should be in print and available, and I have left out those that I cannot recommend. Prices are not listed, as they tend to change.

The Accidental Profession
Education, Training and the People of Publishing
Association of American Publishers, 1977

An Anatomy of Literary Property
By Richard Wincor
Walker & Co., N.Y. 1962
   Far more accessible than his textbook listed above, this can be read with profit by writers and editors alike. Recommended, of course.

The Annotated Alice
By Lewis Carroll, edited by Martin Gardner
Clarkson N. Potter, Inc. N.Y. 1960
Meridian Reprint (Paper)
   This illustrates the point about graphics discussed in the text,

and a copy of this or of any other title in The Annotated series should be looked at by all editors and by any writer who cares about design.

The Art and Science of Book Publishing
By Herbert S. Bailey, Jr.
University of Texas Press, 1970; 1980 (paper)

A very good introduction, highly recommended for young people thinking of going in the business. Bailey's world is much more ordered and sane than what will be found in most trade houses and his ideas are sound. Skip pages 103–173, which are unnecessary and confusing.

Between Covers
The Rise and Transformation of American Book Publishing
By John Tebbel
Oxford University Press, 1987

The one-volume summary of the author's four-volume work, it should only be relied upon up to about 1965. Recommended for the historically minded, but don't expect analysis.

The Blockbuster Complex
Conglomerates, Show Business and Book Publishing
By Thomas Whiteside
Wesleyan University Press, Middletown, Conn., 1981

A good exposition of the current conventional wisdom. Not really out of date. Insiders will know that there is more to it than is presented here, and outsiders should remember that Whiteside is talking only about a layer of icing on the cake, but it's a good place for a beginner to start.

Book Publishing
What It Is, What It Does, 2nd Edition
John P. Dessauer
R. R. Bowker, N.Y. 1981

The basic introduction given to most students. Sound and reliable but dull.

Bibliography

Bookmaking
The Illustrated Guide to Design/Production/Editing
Second Edition
By Marshall Lee
R. R. Bowker, N.Y. 1979
This is *the* book that every editor should know by heart and any serious writer should be aware of. A model of its kind, it cannot be overpraised.

Books
The Culture and Commerce of Publishing
By Lewis A. Coser, Charles Kadushin and Walter W. Powell
Basic Books, N.Y. 1982
A sociological view of publishing based on interviews and questionnaires. My students found it boring and neither very convincing nor particularly illuminating, but it is the only attempt of its kind and should be looked at by beginners.

The Business of Book Publishing
Papers by Practitioners
Edited by Elizabeth A. Geiser and Arnold Dolin,
with Gladys S. Topkis
Westview Press, Boulder, Colo., 1986
My choice as to what a young person should read about the business. Certainly the best book for the beginner who aspires to a career in the field. Elizabeth Sifton's contribution is excellent, and young writers and editors should know it. The book is ridiculously overpriced, so get it at your local library.

The Careful Writer
A Modern Guide to English Usage
By Theodore M. Bernstein
Atheneum, N.Y. 1977
A very valuable guide, and every writer or editor should have it nearby.

The Chicago Manual of Style
13th Edition, Revised and Expanded.

251

By Editorial Staff of the University of Chicago Press,
Chicago, 1982.

Definitive and an absolute necessity for all editors and any
careful writer. All other similar manuals should be considered as
secondary to this.

The Coming of the Book
The Impact of Printing 1450-1800.
By Lucien Febvre and Henri-Jean Martin
NLB, Schocken, N.Y. 1979.

A scholarly book about the early days of printing and bookmaking, very sound on what happened when but not much
concerned about the meaning and social impact. Recommended
for the serious student of history.

The Complete Plain Words
By Sir Ernest Gowers
Revised by Sidney Greenbaum & Janet Whitcut
Introduction by Joseph Epstein
David R. Godine, Boston 1988

Written for the English civil service, this is a wonderful book
and cannot fail to improve the writing of anyone who reads it.

The Concise Oxford Dictionary of Current English
6th Edition, edited by J.B. Sykes
Oxford University Press, Oxford, 1976

Obviously every writer and every editor has to have several
dictionaries, and this one is listed because it seems to me the
handiest, most useful, and least cluttered.

The Copyright Book
A Practical Guide
By William S. Strong
The MIT Press, Cambridge, 3rd Edition, 1990

The best introduction for the generalist. Copyright, however,
can be trickier than it seems, and anyone with any sort of
complicated problem should consult a specialist.

A Dictionary of Modern English Usage
By H. W. Fowler
2nd Edition, revised by Sir Ernest Gowers
Oxford University Press, 1965
  Fowler has fallen out of fashion these days, but I deplore that. Besides the good advice one gets from him, there is always the pleasure in reading anything he has to say. It is not necessary to agree with him all the time in order to write better, and any writer should welcome that.

The Domestication of the Savage Mind
By Jack Goody
Cambridge University Press, N.Y. 1977
  One of my favorite books, this should be read by anyone who wonders where books fit into the larger scheme of things. Suggestive and splendid.

Donnelly Guide to Book Planning
A New Concept in Book Production
R. R. Donnelley & Sons Co.
The Lakeside Press, Chicago, Undated
  This is listed in spite of the fact that it can only be obtained by someone who might order printing from Donnelley and knows a salesman for the company. Other companies have similar planners, and the production department of most publishers should have something like this around. Any editor is well advised to get this and learn to use it, and it wouldn't hurt if writers also looked at it.

Editor to Author
The Letters of Maxwell E. Perkins
Selected and edited with commentary and an introduction by John Hall Wheelock
Charles Scribner's Sons, N.Y., 1950
  The actual letters of the master. Their tact, easy tone and underlying security should be studied by any aspiring editor.

The Elements of Editing
A Modern Guide for Editors and Journalists

By Arthur Plotnik
Macmillan, N.Y., 1982
A very useful introduction for young editors. Recommended.

The Elements of Style
By William Strunk, Jr., and E. B. White
Macmillan, N.Y., 1959
One of the basic, indispensable guides for the writer, and good fun, too. All writers should have it and know it well.

Exercises in Style
By Raymond Queneau
Translated by Barbara Wright
New Directions, N.Y., 1981
A funny, quirky book—ninety-nine mostly useless ways to tell the same trifling anecdote. A puzzler's delight.

Five Hundred Years of Printing
By S. H. Steinberg
Penguin, N.Y. 1974
The leading one-volume account of printing from the beginning, with an emphasis on the history of books. Solid and sound, and recommended for the historically inclined.

The Functions of the Executive
Chester I. Barnard
Harvard University Press, Cambridge, 1968 (Paper)
One of the few, if not the only, really serious and important books for the manager and moneyman. A classic that has lost none of its relevance. Highly recommended.

The Future of the Printed Word
The Impact and Implications of the New Communications Technology
Edited by Philip Hills.
Greenwood Press, Westport, Conn., 1980
Fourteen essays of varying quality, but mostly reassuring to the thoughtful. Marginal but interesting.

Getting into Book Publishing
3rd Edition
By Chandler B. Grannis
R. R. Bowker & Assoc. of American Publishers, N.Y. 1983
  A pamphlet introduction to the subject, including a bibliography and list of relevant courses. Good as far as it goes.

Getting into Print
The Decision-Making Process in Scholarly Publishing
By Walter W. Powell
University of Chicago Press, Chicago, 1985
  A "sharply focused ethnography of big-time academic publishing." Listed here for inclusiveness, but clearly for the specialist.

Getting Published
The Acquisition Process at University Presses
By Paul Parsons
University of Tennessee Press, Knoxville, 1989 (paper)
  Sober, thorough and specialized, this will be illuminating to those in the academic world. Since there is now more than a little overlap of academic and trade publishing, it may well be of use to serious writers outside the universities as well.

The Gutenberg Galaxy
The Making of Typographic Man
By Marshall McLuhan
University of Toronto Press, Toronto, 1962
  If regarded as harmless fun, which is all it ever was, this can still amuse and provoke, but it certainly isn't required reading.

A Handbook for Scholars
By Mary-Claire VanLeunen
"A Complete Guide to the Mechanics of Scholarly Writing: Citation, References, Footnotes, Bibliographies, Format, Styling, Text Preparation, and all related matters."
Knopf, N.Y. 1979
  This is just what it says it is, and the specialist will want to have it.

A History of Book Publishing in the United States
in Four Volumes By John Tebbel
R. R. Bowker Co., N.Y. 1981
Vol. 1 1630–1865
Vol. 2 1865–1919
Vol. 3 1920–1940
Vol. 4 1941–1980

This massive work is as close as anyone is likely to get to a definitive treatment of the subject. It is dry, lacking in a sense of character, and not concerned with larger implications, but, for what it is, I can testify that it does get the facts as straight as they ever can be established. Anyone working in one of the older houses will want to look up the history of that particular house, and should find it here. Reliable and recommended.

How to Be Your Own Literary Agent
The Business of Getting Your Book Published
By Richard Curtis
New Expanded Edition
Houghton Mifflin Co., Boston, 1984 (paper)

A very useful guide for the beginner.

How to Get Happily Published
By Judith Applebaum and Nancy Evans
3rd Edition
Plume. New American Library, N.Y. 1988

This is actually a good book and should be a help to the beginning writer. I do not share the authors' enthusiasm for self-publishing and consider that they are wildly overoptimistic in everything they say about it, especially the financial aspects, but the first half of the book is worth it for any new writer.

Literary Property
By Richard Wincor
Clarkson N. Potter, Inc., N.Y. 1967

Since I published this, clearly I think it is a good and valuable book. Because it deals in basic ideas, it is less out of date now than you might suppose.

The Making of Books
By Sean Jennett
4th Edition, Revised
Praeger, N.Y. 1967
  About printing, binding, design and illustration. Good for what it is.

Max Perkins, Editor of Genius
by A. Scott Berg
Dutton, N.Y. 1978
  The life of the famous Scribner's editor who nurtured Hemingway, Wolfe and Fitzgerald, among plenty of others. Every young editor can profit from this, especially if he takes the trouble to see the strength of determination behind the affable Perkins exterior.

Modern American Usage: A Guide
By Wilson Follett
Hill & Wang, N.Y. 1966
  This should be placed beside Fowler and be ready at hand to any writer or editor who works on text. Less fun than Fowler but probably more useful. A basic necessity.

The Modern Researcher
4th Edition
By Jacques Barzun and Henry F. Graff
Harcourt Brace, Jovanovich, San Diego, Cal., 1985

Newsman's English
By Harold Evans
Holt, N.Y. 1972
  The former editor of the *London Times* and a brilliant intelligence has written a very good book indeed—down-to-earth, practical and useful. It should be much better known than it seems to be and is highly recommended for editors and writers.

On Writing, Editing and Publishing Essays Explicative and Hortatory
By Jacques Barzun

2nd Edition with a foreword by Morris Philipson
University of Chicago Press, Chicago, 1971

On Writing Well:
An Informal Guide to Writing Non-Fiction
By William K. Zinsser
Harper & Row, N.Y. 1980
This is now famous and standard, as it should be. All writers should have it.

One Book/Five Ways
The Publishing Procedures of Five University Presses
Foreword by Joyce Kachergis
Introduction by Chandler Grannis
Afterword by William Kaufmann
William Kaufmann, Inc., Los Altos, Cal.
As discussed in the text, no editor starting out should fail to study this book. It wouldn't hurt if salespeople and money people also contemplated its lessons. It repays close attention and is highly recommended.

The Printing Press as an Agent of Change
Communications and Cultural Transformations in Early-Modern Europe.
By Elizabeth L. Eisenstein
2 volumes.
Cambridge University Press, N.Y. 1979
In my view, a wonderful and important book. I recommend it to thoughtful editors and moneymen, but note that they can and should skip much of the text that devotes itself to matters of religion. Anyone who wants to know whether or not it is worth one's time to work in the book business should read this.

Publishers on Publishing
Selected and Edited with Commentary and Introduction by Gerald Gross.
Prefatory Notes by Frederic G. Melcher

258

Grosset & Dunlap, N.Y. 1961

When this came out, it was one of the few books on the subject and its shortcomings seemed less important. Now it is merely an old collection of thirty-six essays culled mostly from magazines and privately printed books and is of mild historical interest.

The Publishing Game
By Anthony Blond
Jonathan Cape, London 1971

Listed here even though it is probably not obtainable except in London. Blond is very English, gossipy, original, and full of flavor, and any writer or editor who can get it should do so.

Rights Contracts in the Communications Media
By Richard Wincor
2nd Edition
Harcourt Brace, Jovanovich, N.Y. 1982

Wincor is the leading lawyer in the field, and serious students will want this even though it is dry and lawyerlike. For those who need it as a text it is highly recommended. From Ritual to Royalties

Rotten Reviews
A Literary Companion
Edited by Bill Henderson
Introductions by Anthony Brandt
Illustrations by Mary Kornblum
Pushcart Press, Wainscott, N.Y. 1986

Outrageously expensive for what it is, this is nevertheless nice fun even if it seems far too short. A warning and a consolation for all writers and editors, if they feel they need it.

Samuel Johnson and the Impact of Print
By Alvin Kernan
Princeton University Press, Princeton, 1989 (paper)

An account of the first man to make his living as a writer and the beginning of the cultural revolution that this foreshadowed. A readable and interesting book.

A Short History of the Printed Word
By Warren Chappell
Godine, Boston 1980
This is probably the best introduction to alphabets, typography, printing and bookmaking. Handsome itself, it is a pleasant reference for any editor or writer.

Simple and Direct
A Rhetoric for Writers
Revised Edition
Jacques Barzun
Harper & Row, N.Y. 1985
This is the basic nuts and bolts approach to learning how to write, and anyone who wants to learn can improve their techniques by using it. It is the one book every new writer should start with, and all others should follow. Recommended for all writers.

Strictly Speaking
By Edwin Newman
Warner Books, N.Y. 1977
This collection of essays is a delight for all Newman fans, of which I am one. For all authors and editors.

A Style Manual
For Technical Writers and Editors
S. J. Reisman, Editor
Macmillan, N.Y. 1962
This covers technicalities that the regular manual doesn't, and clearly is useful for those who work in those fields.

Technical Writing
Situations and Strategies
By Michael H. Markel

St. Martin's Press, N.Y. 1984

Hard going but worth it for the business writer, scientist or technician.

Thirteen Types of Narratives
A Practical Guide on How to Tell a Story
By Wallace Hildick
Clarkson N. Potter, Inc., N.Y. 1970

As I published this, I think it is useful for the serious writer or for anyone who wants to improve his technique.

The Twentieth-Century Book
Its Illustration and Design
By John Lewis
Reinhold, N.Y. 1967

This is one of many books about graphics and illustration, but it is one of the better ones and has an especially good introduction. Recommended.

The 26 Letters
By Oscar Ogg
Revised Edition
Crowell, N.Y. 1971

A simple and charming history of letters and type. Recommended for the beginner.

A Writer's Guide to Book Publishing
Revised Edition
By Richard Balkin
Hawthorn/Dutton, N.Y. 1981

A very good introduction for the yet to be published writer. Accurate and helpful for what it covers.

The Writer's Lawyer
Essential Legal Advice for Writers and Editors in All Media
By Ronald Goldfarb and Gail E. Ross
Times Books, N.Y. 1989

A very good book indeed. Clear, readable and useful, it should be near at hand in every editorial office.

Index

263

Index

Index

Index